the simple guide to RABBITS

Bobbye Land

t.f.h.

T.F.H. Publications, Inc.

**Special thanks to Rick Clark
for helping me with the research for this book.
You are the best researcher I know and a special friend.**

T.F.H. Publications, Inc.
One TFH Plaza
Third and Union Avenues
Neptune City, NJ 07753

This book has been published with the intent to provide accurate and authoritative information in regard to the subject matter within. While every precaution has been taken in preparation of this book, the publisher and author assume no responsibility for errors or omissions. Neither is any liability assumed for damages resulting from the use of the information herein.

Library of Congress Cataloging-in-Publication Data
Land, Bobbye.
The simple guide to rabbits / Bobbye Land.
p. cm.
Includes index.
ISBN 0-7938-2119-3 (alk. paper)
1. Rabbits as pets. I. Title.
SF453.L36 2004
636.932'2--dc22
2003027380

www.tfh.com

Contents

Should you
Adopt?
Page 47

Where to
place your
rabbit's cage
Page 100

Bath time, Page 107

How to hand-tame your rabbit Page 148

Part One

Bringing a Rabbit Into Your Life

"I don't think this is what the pet store meant
when they said we needed a rabbit hutch."

Choosing the Right Rabbit for You

People have different reasons for choosing a rabbit as a pet. Some choose a rabbit because they want a cute and cuddly companion animal. Others want a rabbit because it is a pet they can enjoy spending time with on a regular basis, and many rabbits come home with owners as impulse purchases. However, the decision to adopt a rabbit as a pet requires as much forethought as the adoption of cats, dogs, or any other animal species–perhaps more, as most people find they were less educated than they thought they were about rabbits when they really begin their research seriously. The issues outlined in this chapter will help you decide whether a rabbit is the right pet for you.

Rabbit ownership comes with many responsibilities.

Rabbits and People: History

Rabbits, also known as lagomorphs, are from the order Lagomorpha. Native populations are found on all continents except Australia and Antarctica, though humans have introduced them to areas on these continents. Rabbits first appeared in recorded human history as early as 1100 B.C., when the Phoenicians landed in Spain and sent messages home about the strange creatures they labeled as "shepan," meaning "one who hides." From their attached drawings, we can assume they were seeing their first rabbits.

However, rabbits did not become an integral part of human life until the 15th century, when French monks devoted considerable time and effort to the selective breeding of wild rabbits to improve their meat and fur production. With these breedings, different color and size mutations appeared and were the beginnings of most of the breeds we recognize today.

Rabbits have not always been well loved throughout history, and certainly even today gardeners shudder when they see a wild rabbit hopping toward their tender lettuce or perennial patches. When rabbits were introduced into both Australia and Chile, the rabbit population became almost a plague. In Chile, the rabbit population endangered the existence of the Patagonian guinea pig, as the massive numbers of rabbits quickly consumed the guinea pigs' usual foods. When rabbits were brought into Antarctica, they flourished with such abandon that they upset the entire balance of nature with the amount of vegetation that they consumed. They existed through the winter months by eating the seaweed that washed ashore. You can also ask any Australian about the "rabbit plague" of the mid-1800s, when rabbits were introduced with disastrous results into an ecosystem that had few predators.

It was in the 1800s that rabbit breeders began getting serious about creating different fancy breeds for the love of the animal as simply a pet. Today, rabbits are still bred for their meat and coats, but they are gaining steadily in popularity as house pets, with more than 15 million rabbits kept as pets in the US alone.

Things To Consider Before Getting a Rabbit

Rabbit ownership is a much bigger step than most people realize. That cute little bundle of fluff and ears is going to become a full-grown rabbit in no time at all and will remain a member of your family for about ten years…or even longer. Don't get a rabbit if you are not certain that you can make a long-term commitment for all aspects of his care. You should be willing to accept responsibility for his health and happiness throughout his entire lifetime, because in return, you will receive unconditional love.

Part 1

The Need for Indoor Housing

Some people mistakenly think of a rabbit as an "outside" pet that lives in a hutch in an obscure part of the yard. Why would someone want a pet that they rarely see and that quickly becomes just another chore to take care of? Certainly rabbits are happiest as house pets, and you will be happier knowing your new buddy is nearby and enjoying the same "creature comforts" that you enjoy yourself. His daily care won't seem a chore if you are doing those things for a pet that is truly part of your family.

Summer and winter temperatures, as well as the constant predator threat, make leaving your bunny outdoors for any length of time unthinkable for any caring pet owner. It is also important to remember that rabbits are social animals requiring either human or fellow rabbit companionship. If you're not going to have time to spend with your bunny cuddling and playing, don't bring him home!

Allergies

If someone in your family has allergies, you should carefully consider your selection of a rabbit as the family pet. A lot of people who are allergic to cats and dogs may find they are not allergic to rabbits, but you should be aware that hay, which is a very important part of a rabbit's diet, can irritate many allergies. Before you bring home a rabbit, discuss it with your doctor or arrange to spend some time with a friend's bunny to see if he or his supplies send you running for antihistamines and tissues.

Size

Be aware that while all baby rabbits are small, cuddly, and cute, not all breeds will stay small (all breeds do, however, stay cuddly and cute). Most adult domestic rabbits are quite a bit larger than wild rabbits, and some breeds will be the size of a cat or small dog (12-15 pounds). You should research the different breeds before you decide to purchase a bunny, and make sure you choose a breed whose adult size and temperament will fit your family's lifestyle, wants, and needs. (See Chapter 2 for descriptions of the different breeds.)

These cute, little ten-week-old Flemish Giants will eventually weigh more than 11 lbs!

Rabbits make great pets for children who learn to respect their cuddly companions.

Bunny Benefits

Want yet another reason to own a bunny? The benefits to your compost pile! You can add the contents of your rabbit's litter box directly to your compost bin. Everything is compostable, even the hair!

Don't worry even if you use sawdust in your bunny pan. The rabbit's urine counteracts the nitrogen-depleting qualities of sawdust. Not only will your plants thank you for the boost to their mulch and potting soil, but you'll also find that you'll have even more earthworms.

Rabbits and Children

One of the most common questions that breeders hear is: "Are your rabbits good with children?" However, what any concerned breeder is going to want to know is: "Are *your children* good with rabbits?" Any child who is going to share a home with a rabbit should have been taught to respect animals. Children should know to never chase or poke their rabbit and to pick him up only occasionally. They should only pick the rabbit up under certain situations, as most rabbits really do not enjoy being held and will only tolerate it occasionally because they like and trust their owner.

Because rabbits communicate solely through their body language (with the exception of a few sounds–some rabbits remain silent their entire lives) your children (and you) should be patient enough to learn their sign language and respect what your rabbit is attempting to say to you.

If a child has been taught to be gentle, caring, quiet, and respectful of your bunny's feelings, then yes, rabbits are very good with children. If your children are loud, boisterous, and refuse to be quiet and gentle with a timid creature, or if they insist on having the rabbit do what they want him to do with no regard to the rabbit's feelings, then, no, sadly, in that instance, rabbits are not good with children.

Even if your children are exactly the type that a bunny can coexist with in a happy relationship, sharing a home with both bunnies and children will create a challenge for you. Furthermore, the younger your children, the greater your challenge will be. It is very hard for small children (preschool age) to differentiate between make-believe and reality. They may find it difficult to understand that their weight can hurt a bunny. After all, they roll over on their stuffed animals at night in their bed and nothing happens. They may also think that feeding part of their snacks

So, Your Child Wants a Rabbit?

Ask yourself these important questions before you say "yes" to your child's frenzied pleas for a rabbit.

√ Do *you* want a rabbit yourself? Remember—although children can make honest promises at the time of purchase that they will take care of the rabbit on a daily basis, once the novelty wears off, it will be up to you to either take care of "bunny duties" or constantly remind your child to do it.

√ Do you realize that it is unacceptable to leave your rabbit confined in a small cage 24/7? A rabbit absolutely must have time to exercise and explore. This means that you will likely need to get used to having a bunny underfoot whether the children are around or not.

√ Are you aware that even the most docile bunny will scratch or nip if he feels threatened, or if he is irritated by too much attention? Can you deal with the fact that at some point your child (or you) may likely receive a scratch from your bunny, and it is unacceptable to punish the rabbit for doing so, as it is only their nature to defend themselves?

√ Is your child willing to be quiet when around the rabbit? To a rabbit, almost everything he encounters is considered a possible predator or something dangerous. Rapid movements and loud sounds will always startle a bunny, even a docile, well-loved, and loveable pet.

√ Are both you and your child aware that rabbits are not intended to be lap pets? Most rabbits don't really like to be picked up and carried around, thought many will tolerate it for short periods of time with people they trust implicitly.

If you answered "no" to any of those questions, it's time to do both some soul-searching and some research. It is likely that another species would be a better pet for your child.

and cookies to their pet is a sign of affection, without realizing that their actions can create a very sick rabbit! It will be up to you to make sure that your children's toys, crayons, chalk, and other potentially dangerous-to-a-rabbit items are picked up and placed out of reach of your curious rabbit.

Spaying and Neutering

Whether you get a male or female rabbit, you should have it sterilized to make it a happier, healthier family pet. Unspayed females are at a very high risk of ovarian, uterine, or mammary cancer, so when your pet female reaches the age of four to six months of age, most veterinarians recommend having her spayed. You will find that males are

Spaying or neutering will make your rabbit a happier, healthier pet.

The Myths

Beware of the following misconceptions regarding rabbits and their care. Though these myths are common, they are just that—myths. It will be your responsibility as a rabbit owner to know the facts.

Myth: Rabbits are low-maintenance, easy-to-care-for pets.

Fact: Although he won't have to be walked every day like a dog, a rabbit still requires daily maintenance. His cage must be kept clean, his litter pan emptied often, and his food and water dish should be kept clean and filled properly. Rabbits also require regular grooming.

Myth: Rabbits only live a year or two, so it's not a long-term relationship.

Fact: Rabbits can live eight to ten years or even longer with proper care.

Myth: With a rabbit, you won't have a vet bill like you do for dogs and cats.

Fact: Rabbits need medical attention just like every other living creature for routine health care and emergency treatment.

Myth: Rabbits are actually happier living outside in their very own hutch.

Fact: Would you want to live away from all social activity in a solitary and lonesome environment? Neither do they.

Myth: Rabbits are very nasty creatures and have a bad body odor.

Fact: Quite the opposite. Rabbits are very clean creatures that bathe themselves more regularly than humans. They take great pains not to soil their bedding, and neither their body nor their droppings have an offensive odor.

Myth: Rabbits can exist quite nicely on a diet of processed rabbit pellets.

Fact: Rabbits need hay in their diet to maintain a healthy digestive system. They also need a variety of fruits and vegetables to stay healthy.

much easier to care for if they are neutered, as you will be able to avoid unwanted spraying as well as the risk of testicular cancer. Males can be neutered at a slightly earlier age than females–usually between three to four months of age.

Spaying or neutering your pet will also avoid a lot of hormonally induced spats between rabbits of the same sex, as well as eliminate the possibility of a litter of unwanted babies. If you have two rabbits of the opposite sex, be aware that they mature much more rapidly than other species, and your female will be capable of bearing babies well before she is six months of age.

Cost Concerns

Although the price tag for a rabbit may not be as high as that for a purebred cat or dog, the cost of a bunny's upkeep can equal that of either. You should consider the cost of spaying or neutering your rabbit, and realize that litter for his box can cost about twice the amount of what is necessary for cats. You will also want to feed a good-quality food that is of adequate nutrition for continued good health, as well as tasty and nutritional treats. Rabbits will be just as happy with homemade "freebie" toys as they will be with purchased toys, but most people can't pass up buying a few treats and toys when they visit the pet store for food and other necessary supplies. Cages can also be expensive, depending on the size and quality of workmanship.

Barring emergencies, vet costs should be biannual for checkups and vaccinations. Emergencies and accidents can quickly cost into the triple and even quadruple digits! As a pet owner, you should have a separate emergency fund to take care of unexpected vet costs so as to be able to give your pet every opportunity to receive adequate health care if needed. By the time you have added up all the costs, that free or low-cost bunny becomes a serious budget item—one that you should be certain you can afford or want badly enough to readjust your budget accordingly, before you bring him home.

Consider the costs involved with owning a rabbit before you buy one.

What Type of Rabbit is Right for You?

Once you've made the decision to bring a rabbit into your home as a pet, you need to make sure to get the *right* rabbit for you and your family. It's very easy to be charmed by the first fluffy rabbit you see in a pet store window, but it is very important to take the proper consideration before you pull out your wallet.

During this search, you may be offered animals that are unhealthy, older, or have temperament problems. Remember that the pet you choose will be part of your life for many years, and you owe it to yourself and your family to start out with a pet that is as

Am I Ready to be a Rabbit Parent?

Do the following statements apply to you?

√ I have extra time each day that I would like to spend with a pet, playing, cuddling, or just being together.

√ I have room in my budget to cover not only daily expenses but unexpected medical bills as well.

√ I have room in my house for a very large cage, and I have no other pets that would harm a bunny (or I have a way to keep them away from my bunny when he is out of his cage.)

√ I can be patient with a pet even when he does bad things, realizing that I am usually at fault for his transgressions, as I allowed the circumstances that, in turn, allowed him to be bad.

√ My children are very responsible and will accept taking care of the rabbit's needs as part of their daily chores.

√ I am patient enough to take the time to train my new rabbit to use his litter box, and I am willing to clean up any accidents until that time, without losing my temper at my rabbit; I realize he is doing the best he can.

If this sounds like you, and you feel that you can provide everything a rabbit needs to stay happy and healthy, you are very ready to open your heart and your home to a new rabbit!

A rabbit should be at least eight weeks old when you purchase him.

sound as possible in both body and mind. To that end, there are some general criteria that you should follow without exception to ensure that the rabbit you choose is healthy, happy, and able to share your life for many, many years.

Age

Unless the rabbit you are considering has been a family pet and is well used to being handled and loved, it is best to acquire a rabbit between the ages of 8 and 12 weeks, when he will be easier to handle and tame. He will be old enough to be on his own but young enough to have a pliable personality.

You should never purchase a bunny that is younger than eight weeks old because until this point, a baby rabbit is too young to be away from his mother. Although rabbit mothers do not nurture their babies constantly the way other small mammals do, a bunny does learn behavior patterns from his mother, as well as receive nourishment. A bunny that is younger than eight weeks old may be able to survive without his mother, but he will not thrive or reach his standard size, because he will not be used to eating solid foods. He may also feel lonesome because he's away from his mother and his brothers and sisters. By not purchasing a bunny that is younger than eight weeks old, you can make sure your rabbit gets the best start he can have in life.

Coat Condition

The coat should be clean and healthy-looking with no dandruff, which is a sign of mites, or bare patches, which can be indicative of mites, other external parasites, or perhaps skin irritations or allergies. If you are choosing an older rabbit, it is possible that he might be in the middle of a molt, which can make him look pretty ratty. A good rabbit professional can explain this to you and show you how to groom the bunny to make the molting go faster, so he can quickly return to his normal beautiful self. Even in molt, a rabbit's skin should be in good condition because only the dead hair falls out; by doing so, patches of new, plush hair growth are left behind, never bald spots where you can see the skin.

Colors

Choosing the color of your new rabbit is a decision based solely on your own personal likes and dislikes. Just as one man's trash is another man's treasure, one man's "plain old white rabbit" may be a "snowy princess" in the eyes of another. Because rabbits come in such a rainbow of colors and a myriad of patch and spot patterns, you are certain to find one

Minimum Age

Although bunnies mature quite rapidly and may appear old enough to be weaned from their mother, be certain that the bunny you choose is a minimum of eight weeks of age. If the rabbit is any younger than that, you could be facing health problems as your rabbit matures.

A bunny can indeed *exist* when taken away from his mother at an earlier age, but he will not age and mature as gracefully as a rabbit that is allowed to stay with his mother and siblings for the suggested length of time. He will likely not have the "social graces" of a rabbit that has learned a few of life's lessons from a loving mother.

Rabbits are available in a wide variety of colors.

that is marked to suit your preference. Although some breeds come in only specific colors and color placements, there is virtually something for everyone–small bunnies with spots, large bunnies with freckles, and even larger, snow-white bunnies. Take your time, do your homework, and you'll find exactly the rabbit to suit your taste.

Environment and Living Conditions

The most important aspect of choosing your rabbit is to purchase him from someone you trust. It is far better, easier, and less expensive to avoid illness and bad health in your rabbit than to cure it later. It is believed that well over half of all rabbit ailments are caused completely or at least in great part by poor husbandry. Drafty accommodations, unclean food and water dishes, contaminated or poor-quality foods, overcrowding, lack of adequate exercise, and poor breeding practices can not only cause disease, but spread it. You should be sure that your rabbit was born, raised, and is now being kept in as good a situation as possible to ensure his continued good health.

Hair Length and Type

Rabbits come in two different hair types: longhaired and shorthaired. Longhaired rabbits will require quite a bit of grooming and brushing on a regular basis to keep them from becoming a matted mess. Shorthaired rabbits will need an occasional grooming to avoid shedding hair in the house, but if grooming is neglected a bit, the bunny won't suffer. A longhaired rabbit's health, however, can be compromised if his grooming is neglected. Unless you really enjoy wielding a brush and comb on a daily basis, or at least several times a week, you should choose a rabbit with a short or plush coat.

Although the longer-haired rabbits, such as the Angoras, make excellent pets and are beautiful animals, they do require a lot of time and effort to maintain those gorgeous coats. Angoras that are neglected for any considerable length of time become matted messes that may have to be shaved down to the skin to restart hair growth. Don't take on the responsibility of coat care if you aren't going to have time to manage it and aren't going to enjoy the chore. Shorter-haired bunnies are just as beautiful in their own way; some, such as the Rex, have coats that are as unique and attractive as the longhaired breeds.

Health

Always handle a rabbit before purchasing him, and check him thoroughly for any obvious health problems. Don't trust yourself to make a final decision as to his health; however, take him to a vet as soon as possible for a thorough checkup. Never choose a sick rabbit as a pet because you feel sorry for him. Start out with a healthy rabbit that will be able to give your family years of enjoyment. Purchasing a sickly rabbit may make you feel that you're doing a good deed, but you're setting yourself up for not only the possibility of large vet bills, but the grief of losing a pet you've come to care about, long before his time should have come. Some breeds are more prone to certain health problems, and this should be one of the first questions you ask the breeder when inquiring about those particular breeds.

You should make certain that the rabbit you choose is in tip-top condition. The eyes should

Make sure the rabbit you select is healthy.

The Healthy Rabbit Checklist

To ensure that you have chosen a rabbit that is as healthy as possible, complete the following checklist:

1. Did you purchase your rabbit from someone who is a rabbit expert, someone you trust, and someone who can assure you that your rabbit was born and raised in healthy, humane conditions?

2. Did you choose a rabbit that is at least eight weeks of age, one that has not been separated from his mother for longer than a very few days? Remember that the baby bunny you choose from a pet store was not born there and likely didn't just arrive that day. If he is eight weeks old now, it is likely he was taken away from his mother up to two weeks earlier. Ask questions, and be sure you are getting honest answers.

3. If you chose an older rabbit, did you get his veterinary records or a statement of health from a veterinarian?

4. Did you receive any sort of health guarantee in writing (genetic as well as overall)?

5. If your rabbit is supposed to be purebred, did you receive a copy of his pedigree?

6. Did you check the rabbit closely for wounds or any signs of illness?

7. Are your rabbit's teeth aligned correctly?

8. Is his bottom clean and dry?

9. Could you hold your bunny? Was he calm and obviously used to being handled by humans?

10. Does his weight appear average—not too little, not too much?

Your Bunny's Past

It's not enough to know that your rabbit is in good surroundings now. Make sure that he was born in humane conditions and that his birth was planned by people who breed carefully, with thoughtful consideration of all factors.

The Eyes, Ears, and Nose Have It

In choosing your new bunny, remember that you can learn a lot from looking at its eyes, ears, and nose. The eyes should be clear without any discharge. The ears should be pink and free of any waxy buildup. The nose should be free of discharge or excessive moisture. To be sure the bunny isn't just a very good groomer, check the inside of his front paws to see that he hasn't wiped his nose or eyes on his "sleeve."

be bright and clear, not runny or encrusted with dried matter. The nose, too, should be clean with no dried mucus present. The ears should be pink, but not red, and clean inside without any appearance of waxy buildup, especially a dark or black wax that can be indicative of an ear mite infestation.

Very slowly and carefully, place your head against the rabbit's chest; his breathing should be quiet with no rattling sounds evident. Rabbits should have a good amount of fat and flesh covering their bone structure. Their backbone should not be prominent. Run your hands over the rabbit in the direction that his hair grows and see if he feels well nourished. He should not be overly fat, however, as this might denote too much time spent in an area where he could not get enough exercise. There should be no swellings, lumps, or bumps beneath the skin or on the skin.

You should always check the teeth of any rabbit you are considering purchasing (as well as the teeth of his parents if you are considering breeding your pet in the future). The top teeth should slightly overlap the bottom ones, and they should not appear overly long. There should be no sign of decay evident. Wet or matted fur on the chin can indicate a health problem or dental trouble.

The correct term for a rabbit's bottom is the "vent." You should have a quick look at the vent area to see that it is clean and shows no sign of dried feces or any signs of current diarrhea.

Male or Female?

Rabbits are social animals and will appreciate being given a companion whenever possible. Littermates may be kept together, but they should be neutered if they are of opposite sexes. Unrelated females will sometimes fight to the death if they are kept in close quarters. Uncastrated males will often fight each other even if littermates. Unless you have a great outlet for forever-homes for pet bunnies that you produce, you should never attempt to keep two rabbits of the opposite sex together. All the jokes about how fast rabbits multiply are based on serious facts. They breed often and usually with great success, and two bunnies can quickly reproduce into several dozens.

Rabbits will appreciate having a companion, but they should be spayed or neutered first.

Both sexes have been known to spray their urine to mark their territory, although an unneutered buck is going to be worse about it than any other rabbit.

Purebred or Mutt?

Just as with any other species, you can be more certain of what you are getting if you choose a purebred animal. Knowing your rabbit's ancestry helps you know what to expect as far as size, temperament, hair type, etc. as your rabbit matures. (Detailed descriptions of different rabbit breeds are provided in Chapter 2.) However, a mutt rabbit (known in the rabbit world as "scrubs") whose ancestry is uncertain can still give you just as many years of love and companionship as a purebred bunny. It's up to you. Beauty is truly in the eye of the beholder. If a mixed-breed rabbit catches your eye and captures your heart, and you have no aspirations toward breeding or exhibiting your pet, then make your choice knowing that you have found a "custom-made" and unique bunny that's just right for *you*!

Spaying and Neutering

Although littermates of the opposite sex will not fight each other if housed together, one or the other or both will have to be spayed or neutered to avoid un-wanted pregnancies.

Show Rabbit Vs. Pet Rabbit

Unless you're going to become involved in actually showing your rabbit, there's no need to hold out for a "show-quality" bunny. In

Mixed-breed rabbits, like this one, equal show rabbits in terms of pet quality.

It's All in the Name

A male rabbit is called a buck, while a female rabbit is called a doe (yes, just like deer). When they're sterilized, bucks get neutered, does get spayed. A baby bunny is called a kit, short for kitten.

fact, most of the time the difference between one that is deemed a "pet" and one that is declared a "show" animal, may be something as paltry as a misplaced spot or freckle or a few ounces or inches. Many times, the problem that keeps an animal from being show quality may be something that you will find unique and interesting (one ear stands while one ear droops, eyes of two different colors, unique markings, etc.). No one except a true rabbit professional will know the difference between a show animal and a pet. (Well, except possibly for your accountant, as show rabbits usually carry a higher price tag than pets.) Furthermore, there is no difference in the temperament between a show rabbit and a pet.

If you think there is a chance that you or someone in your family might be interested in attending and getting involved in rabbit shows, there is no reason not to go ahead and purchase the highest quality rabbit you can find as a pet. Don't be surprised if the breeder insists that you either show the rabbit yourself or have someone else do it for you, and they may make you put your agreement to do so in writing. Remember, they've invested a lot of time, energy, and money in producing the highest quality rabbits they can, and they want the show world to see the results of their efforts. Be honest with them if you're not sure about showing but would like to keep the option open, and you will likely still get a very high-quality rabbit that will be competitive at shows should you decide to undertake the endeavor.

Size

If you live in a large house and plan on spending a lot of time with your rabbit, you can live comfortably with one of the giant breeds. If you're living in an apartment, small house, or motor home, however, one of the dwarf breeds was likely designed with people like you in mind. Size is one of the most important decisions when choosing a rabbit. Some bunnies are far more than a lapful, while others can sit comfortably on one hand. In the middle are

Part 1

the standard-sized rabbits that fit the profile of the mental image that most people have of a rabbit.

Because rabbits come in sizes from just a few pounds to up to 15 pounds (or larger, depending on their feeding and exercise program), you are certain to find one that fits your needs and desires. Just be sure that you choose your bunny from someone you can trust. You don't want to leave the store with a "guaranteed Dwarf bunny" that grows to a whopping 14 pounds, and you don't want to watch as your "giant breed" stops growing at 5 pounds. Do enough research to know what you want, then research the person from whom you expect to purchase your rabbit until you are sure that they know what they are talking about and you will indeed be getting what you pay for.

Temperament and Behavior

You should spend as much time as possible observing any rabbit you are considering purchasing. He should move freely with no sign of stiffness or lameness. His feet should be in good shape, tight and clean, with no calluses on his footpads (a warning signal that he has been kept in a cage with improper flooring). He should appear alert, healthy, and interested in his surroundings. He should accept a treat from you and be curious about the sounds and activities around him–but not scared. If he looks very apprehensive, stressed, or sits hunched in a corner ignoring what goes on around him, you should consider a different rabbit or perhaps come back another day to see if he has calmed down when he becomes familiar with his surroundings, especially if he just arrived in a pet shop or has been traveling.

From the time they are a few weeks old, pet rabbits should experience human handling.

Any rabbit that is being offered for sale as a pet should have been handled since he was just a few weeks old. He should be well used to being picked up, handled, and petted. He should not be afraid of people, although he cannot be faulted for being frightened if strangers are loud or boisterous. You should be very quiet and not make any sudden movements around any rabbit until he is well accustomed to you and

Get a rabbit that will fit your family's personality and lifestyle.

feels secure with you. Children should be reminded to be quiet and patient with rabbits because, to a rabbit, even a small child is a giant and therefore a potential predator.

If your bunny is going to be a house rabbit, it's a good idea to spend some time with him loose with you in a safe area to see how he reacts to new situations. He should be curious about you but also willing to check out his new surroundings as well.

Careful consideration of all these aspects of the mental and physical health of your potential bunny can ensure that you will have a happy, healthy pet to share your life for many years to come.

Be sure that you get a rabbit that has a temperament that will fit your personality and your family's lifestyle. If you want a quiet bunny that will enjoy sitting on your lap while you watch TV and that will enjoy spending time quietly with you, don't choose one of the breeds that are known for their higher energy levels. If you know your pet will only have a limited amount of time outside his cage, don't choose a pet that will fret and possibly do damage to himself or to his surroundings. Instead, choose a breed that is known for its docile temperament and social behavior.

If your family is high-energy, however, and you have children that will enjoy playing frequently with the rabbit, a docile, laid-back rabbit is going to be overwhelmed by all the activity. Thinking ahead of time as to what you can offer the rabbit in terms of social time can help make your decision easier. Almost any breed can be hand tamed, but some crave more human interaction than others, some are more playful, while others are docile and will put up with a little neglect that would send others into a chewing frenzy. Again, do your homework and ask breeders a lot of questions. Then, listen carefully to their answers and make your decisions accordingly.

Now that you know what kind of rabbit you would like to bring into your home—it's time to pick the breed!

Rabbit Breeds

It is estimated that there are more than 100 different breeds of rabbits, though many breeds are only available in their country of origin. Not to worry—no matter where you are, there will certainly be a wide enough array of breeds from which to choose. There are also different varieties within the breeds. A rabbit's shape, features, or coat defines his particular breed, while variety is determined by color variations found within the breed itself. Some individual breeds of rabbits were once, in fact, just a variety of another breed, but they developed to the point where they have their own standard and thus their own breed.

There are more than 100 different breeds of rabbits in the world.

Part 1

A breed standard describes specific characteristics that a rabbit must possess.

Breed Standards

Each country sets a "standard" for each breed that is exhibited within its boundaries; this standard becomes a blueprint that breeders use when choosing their breeding stock. How a rabbit conforms to his breed standard will determine whether or not he can be shown. Each standard is based on an allocation of 100 points per animal, with those points divided between the features that make that breed unique and those that are important to its appearance.

Once you have decided on a breed of rabbit, you should acquire the standard for that breed so that you will know the quality of the animal you purchase and how closely it adheres to the way the breed club intends it to look. Be aware that many rabbits that make their way to pet shops and other animal vendors may not be purebred, although their "tag" may state them as such. Certainly a "mutt" rabbit is just as loving and irresistible a pet as his purebred cousins, but if you should become involved in showing, there will be no classes in which he can compete because there are no classes for mixed-breed rabbits at any show. Also, you cannot be sure of the adult weight or size of a baby bunny if you cannot be certain he was bred to the standard for his particular breed.

Rabbit breeds are divided into two main groups that classify them based on whether they were developed for their fur or as utility breeds. Rabbits in both groups come in a myriad of shapes and sizes and a rainbow of colors. One is destined to be the one for you–just take your time and make certain you are making an informed choice. Do your homework and learn as much as possible about the different breeds. Visit a rabbit show and talk to breeders of different breeds and varieties. There are many websites that list upcoming shows in your area.

Purchasing Rabbits at Shows

If you think you might purchase a rabbit at the show, be sure you go prepared. Although there are usually crates and cages for sale, there may not be, and you don't want to run the risk of finding the perfect bunny and not having a way to get him home. Take a container of clean, fresh water, a plastic bag of rabbit food, and a handful of hay. A carrot or other healthy treat will also go a long way toward helping you make friends with your new pet.

Rabbit shows are daylong adventures, so take along a folding chair and a small notebook for taking notes about the various breeds, as well as for jotting down contact information from different breeders. Be sure to ask when you walk up to someone in the exhibition area if they have time to talk before you start your conversation, and plan a time to come back later if they are unable to talk at that moment. For most people, bunny shows are a time of "hurry up and wait," and although they may be in a rush to get their rabbit before a judge in time for judging, the actual judging goes quite quickly, and then they may have several hours to kill before they are needed again, and they will welcome your company as they wait.

Many people will have baby bunnies at the show for sale. Don't assume that just because someone is at a show that they are dedicated to producing healthy pets or that they even know what they are doing. Talk to a lot of people, compare notes, and see for yourself how the bunnies are caged. Be aware that traveling cages for rabbits are very small and cramped, but they should not live in those crates when they are at home. You should also make sure that the exhibitor's area is kept clean. Make sure the rabbits' feet are not stained and dirty, the ears are clean, and the eyes bright and shiny.

It is also a good idea to ask breeders the following questions:

- How are your rabbits maintained at your home?

- How many rabbits do you house?

Rabbit Breed Standards Around the World

Although rabbits are fairly the same much the world over, the standards do differ somewhat between those set forth by the ARBA and rabbit breeder associations in other countries. As time goes by, breeders begin to alter breeds slightly to cater to current whims, sometimes creating entirely new breeds.

Perhaps the biggest difference in rabbit breeding and showing occurs on the show table. European rabbit associations take a different approach to classifying and judging rabbits than what is practiced in North America. Rather than evaluating each rabbit against another rabbit, they set forth a standard against which each animal is judged on his own merits.

• How often do you breed your does?

• Are your baby rabbits handled from an early age to make them more receptive to human hands?

• How long do your baby rabbits stay with their mother and siblings?

• What formula or food do you use to wean your baby rabbits? What should I continue to feed my new rabbit?

• Why did you choose the breed of rabbit you have? Why do you think it is the right one for me?

• If this rabbit doesn't work out, will you take him back?

• If I decide to show or breed my rabbit, can I count on you for professional advice?

• Do you provide a pedigree with your rabbits?

Always ask questions. Move along if you find a breeder who doesn't want to answer them. A good, dedicated, and concerned breeder will want to find good, responsible, forever homes for the babies he or she produces and will be eager to teach you all you will need to know to enable you to provide a safe and happy environment for your new pet.

If you find that you enjoy the show situation and think you might like to show your bunny, be sure and tell the breeder that. He or she might have a young hopeful available that he or she wasn't planning to offer to a pet home. However, don't use the possibility of showing the rabbit as a ploy to get a "better bunny."

Check out all the breeds, from the dwarfs to the giants, and

Before purchasing a rabbit at a show, ask the breeder lots of questions.

Show Me

Rabbit shows make excellent daylong outings for the entire family. Pack a picnic lunch, carry along some lawn chairs, and prepare to be amazed at all the different breeds of rabbits. Although there will be baby bunnies at the show, don't be swayed by a wriggly nose and bright eyes. All baby bunnies are cute! Do your homework and find the breed that is right for you and your family.

Ask the breeders and exhibitors questions (when you are certain they have time to talk to you) and learn as much as possible about your chosen breed before you start choosing the individual rabbit. Don't assume that because someone is showing his or her rabbits that they have some sort of "seal of approval."

Look closely to see how well maintained the rabbits are, as well as what condition their show cages and their setup are kept. Even if you decide not to show your rabbit later on, you should keep a contact in the "rabbit world" so you can find out about upcoming rabbit events, as most are excellent places to find rabbit supplies that aren't available elsewhere.

give each of them a chance to steal your heart. Both size groups have their advantages, and the breeders of each will be happy to point them out to you and help you come to a decision as to what will best suit your situation.

Size Does Matter

Rabbits come in sizes ranging from those that would fit into your pocket to some that look as if they would require a wheelbarrow or baby carriage to carry around. There is no right or wrong choice when deciding what rabbit will best fit your lifestyle. Follow your heart–just be sure that you are well educated in all aspects of rabbit ownership before you make your final decision. Size is one of the most important aspects of choosing your new family pet. There are estimated to be more than 100 rabbit breeds, but the following sections describe some of the most common rabbit breeds that are purchased as pets.

Small/Dwarf Rabbit Breeds

If you live in an apartment, small house, condominium, or are tooling around the country in a motor home, nothing could be more fitting than one of the dwarf breeds. Dwarf rabbits all have one thing in common: All of them will tip the scales at 5 pounds or less.

The American Fuzzy Lop weighs about 3 lbs and has dense, slightly coarse wool.

American Fuzzy Lop

American Fuzzy Lop bucks weigh about 3 pounds, with slightly larger does. Like the Wooly, the Fuzzy Lop was originated in the US by crossing the Holland Lop and the Angora. The wool of the American Lop is very dense, slightly coarse, and is approximately 2 inches long. It requires frequent grooming to remain unmatted.

Britannia Petite

The Britannia Petite is slender and fine-boned, and as the name implies, originated in England, where it was for many years the smallest of all the dwarf breeds. They tend to be a little more lively and high-strung than other breeds, and careful research should be done before choosing this breed as a family pet, especially for a first-time rabbit owner. Their coats come in black, black otter, chestnut, sable martin, and ruby-eyed white.

Rabbit Sizes and Breeds

The following list describes the different size categories of rabbits and which breeds fit into those categories.

Small/Dwarf—2 to 6 lbs	Medium—6 to 9 lbs	Large—9 to 11 lbs	Giant—11 lbs and over
American Fuzzy Lop	American Sable	American	Checkered Giant
Britannia Petite	Belgian Hare	American Chinchilla	Flemish Giant
Dutch	English Angora	Beveren	(Patagonian)
Dwarf Hotot	English Spot	Californian	French Lop
Florida White	French Angora	Champagne d'Argent	Giant Chinchilla
Havana	Harlequin	Cinnamon	
Himalayan	Lilac	Crème d'Argent	
Holland Lop	Rex	English Lop	
Jersey Wooly	Rhinelander	Giant Angora	
Mini Lop	Satin Angora	Hotot	
Mini Rex	Silver Marten	New Zealand	
Netherland Dwarf	Standard Chinchilla	Palomino	
Polish		Satin	
Silver		Silver Fox	
Tan			

Dutch

The Dutch rabbit, with his "panda bear" appearance in coloring, is the heaviest and probably the most recognizable of the small-breed rabbits. This is one of the oldest of the domesticated rabbit breeds, with records placing it in England (from its home country of Holland) in the early 1800s. There are six colors of Dutch rabbit, including black, blue, gray, chocolate, steel, yellow, and tortoise, each of them with the distinctive white saddle, face, blaze, and feet. The markings in the Dutch rabbit standard are very specific. The line between the self color and white must be very sharp and as straight as possible. The white blaze should go to a "V" at the base of the ears. The white on the rear feet should extend only an inch and a quarter and should end in a straight line.

A full-grown Dutch rabbit should never weigh more than 5 pounds, but many of them get very close to that adult weight. Most Dutches have very good temperaments, being easygoing and easily trained. They make a very good choice for the first-time rabbit owner.

Dwarf Hotot

Looking as if he is wearing eyeliner, the Dwarf Hotot is an easily recognizable breed of bunny. Always white with the distinctive black spot around his eye, the Hotot weighs about 3 pounds at maturity. His larger cousin, the Blanc De Hotot, looks identical except for the fact that he weighs in at more than 8 pounds.

Florida White

The Florida White was developed in Florida by crossing Dutch, Polish, and New Zealand White rabbits. The breed is small, with a small head and short ears.

Havana

The fur of the Havana is a rich, shiny, dark brown with dark-brown eyes. This rabbit is small but has a healthy build, weighing around 4½ to 6½ pounds. The three recognized color varieties are black, blue, and chocolate.

White coloring and a black spot around the eye characterize the Dwarf Hotot.

Himalayan

Himalayan rabbits are considered to be one of the more docile rabbit breeds. They can be traced back for centuries, and the breed is one of the few rabbit breeds that was not created by crossing other rabbit breeds. Weighing 2 to 4 pounds, the "Himmy" (as he is known to the fancy) comes in five varieties: black, blue, chocolate, lilac, and white with colored markings (such as those of a Himalayan cat).

Holland Lop

The smallest of the lop-eared breeds is the Holland Lop, which should weigh no more than 4 pounds and ideally will weigh around 3 pounds. This is a fairly new breed to the US, having only been recognized by the American Rabbit Breeder's Association (ARBA) since 1980. Their long, floppy ears make them a favorite with pet owners. The recognized colors of Holland Lop are agouti, broken, pointed white, self, shaded, and ticked.

Jersey Wooly

The Mini Rex's plush fur comes in many colors, such as the lilac pictured here.

Another rabbit with a distinctive look is the Jersey Wooly. Developed in the 1970s in the US (in New Jersey, as one would suspect from the name), the Wooly is one of the smaller rabbits, weighing no more than $3\frac{1}{2}$ pounds. The fur of the Jersey Wooly is similar to the French Angora but is non-matting and should be between 2 to 3 inches in length. The fur can be agouti, self, shaded, and tan patterned. The Jersey Wooly is a very gentle and sweet rabbit and makes an excellent pet.

Mini Lop

The Mini Lop is a smaller version of the French Lop and has a thick, stocky build. This rabbit weighs about $4\frac{1}{2}$ to $6\frac{1}{2}$ pounds and is recognized in solid or broken varieties.

Mini Rex

It only takes one touch to know what makes the Mini Rex different from any of the other dwarf rabbit breeds. Their coat (identical to the coat of the larger Standard Rex rabbit) is short, plushy, and velvety-soft, unlike any

Part 1

other fur. This breed is known for its cuddling and docile temperament. The Mini Rex is one of the heavier of the dwarf breeds at 4 to 4½ pounds. As with most breeds, the does are slightly larger than the bucks. The Mini Rex comes in the same colors as his larger cousin – black, blue, broken (large spots of color broken with large amounts of white), castor, chinchilla, chocolate, Himalayan, lilac, lynx, opal, red, seal, tortoise, and white.

Netherland Dwarf

On the other end of the weight scale is the Netherland Dwarf. As the name implies, this breed originated in the Netherlands. The desired adult weight is between 2 and 2½ pounds. They are found in almost every known color of rabbit, with 24 of those colors recognized by the ARBA. The Netherland Dwarf is the breed most commonly found through show breeders.

The Netherland Dwarf is the breed mostly commonly found through show breeders.

Polish

The American Polish rabbit is a dwarf breed that should never exceed 2½ to 3 pounds. The ARBA accepts Polish rabbits in the following colors: black, blue, broken, chocolate, and white. White Polish may be either blue or ruby eyed. The Polish rabbit is oftentimes confused with the Netherland Dwarf, although upon close comparison, you will find that the Polish's ears are not as long as the Netherland Dwarf's, and their faces are not as round.

Silver

The fur of the Silver has pigment-free tips, giving the fur an appearance of a silver color. This rabbit weighs 4 to 7 pounds and comes in three varieties: brown, fawn, and gray.

Tan (or Black and Tan)

This rabbit originated in England, and bucks weigh 4 to 5½ pounds, while does weigh 4 to 6 pounds. Despite his name, the Tan rabbit is also found in blue, chocolate, and lilac, each with distinctive tan points on the toes and as a narrow ring around the eyes and nostrils.

Mid-Sized Rabbit Breeds (Medium)

The medium or mid-sized rabbit breeds are slightly larger than dwarf/small rabbits, weighing approximately 6 to 9 pounds. Some of the most endearing rabbit breeds fall into a mid-sized category.

American Sable

The American Sable is a gorgeous deep brown, with darker ears, face, legs, and tail. Looking much like his namesake, the American Sable was created as a fur rabbit, not valued as a family pet. This breed averages 9 pounds.

Color-Coded

The following is a short glossary of color terms as recognized by the ARBA.

Agouti: A coloring in which each individual hair shaft has three or more bands of color, usually darker at the base. True agouti can be determined by blowing on the coat. If the hair parts and shows a bull's-eye at the center of the part, it is an agouti coat. Agouti colors include chestnut, chinchilla, and lynx.

Broken: Any recognized color in conjunction with white and carrying the breed pattern for spotting.

Castor: A rich chestnut-brown tipped in black.

Pointed white: A variety where the body of the rabbit is white, and the ears, nose, feet, and tail are darker (like that of a Himalayan or Siamese cat).

Self: The same color over all the body.

Shaded: A rabbit with a gradual transition of the same color, with darker color on head, ears, tail, and feet.

Steel: Very dark-chocolate brown with tips of gold or silver.

Tan Pattern (or "points"): Where the surface color of the head, outside the head, front of the forefeet, outside the hind feet, top, and sides of the body are one specific color, with a designated undercolor on the underside.

Ticking: Drops of any dark color against a background of white, giving the effect of pepper mixed into salt.

Belgian Hare

Weighing from 6 to 9½ pounds, the Belgian Hare is a reddish-tan or chestnut with slate-blue undercoloring. He has a slender build, and his coat is stiffer than other breeds.

Chinchilla (Standard)

The Chinchilla rabbit, weighing in at around 6 pounds, was originally from France, where the breed rapidly gained in popularity because of its floppy ears, luxurious, short, dense fur, and lovely coloring. The Chinchilla was named as such because of his resemblance to the South American chinchilla. This breed has the unique hair coloration of dark, slate-blue underfur, pearl edged with black midlayer of coat, and light-gray ticked with a white top coat. Other colors have been developed over time, including Blue, Iron Gray, and Brown varieties. The Chinchilla breed has been used in improving the fur of many other rabbit breeds.

The Belgian Hare has a slender build and a reddish-tan or chestnut coat.

English, French, and Satin Angoras

Among the medium-sized group of rabbit breeds, there are three different breeds of Angora rabbits: English, French, and Satin. The English Angora is the most popular of the Angora breeds and is easily recognizable as it has soft, cottony hair all over, including the body, head, paws, and even the ears. They are the smallest Angora breed, weighing 5 to 8 pounds. Although they are beautiful to look at when they are well groomed, none of the Angora breeds are a good pet choice for someone who dislikes pet grooming, as they require constant brushing to avoid matting. Angora wool, plucked and not shorn if possible, is among the most prized of fibers for weavers, with the wool of the French Angora being in higher demand by hand spinners.

The French Angora, which weighs 8 to 10 pounds, has less long hair on the head, face, and feet than the English Angora and more guard hair; therefore, these rabbits require a little less time for grooming. However, they still have a higher grooming requirement than any of the regular coated breeds.

Part 1

The Satin Angora is a fairly new variety bred specifically for its satiny coat.

The Satin Angora is a fairly new variety bred specifically for its satiny coat. This variety requires less maintenance grooming than any of the Angora breeds and is just between the sizes of the other two medium Angora breeds, weighing 6 to 9 pounds.

All three of these Angora breeds have coats of white as well as other solid colors, although the English coat colors lack the depth of color that the French and Satin have.

English Spot

The English Spot weighs between 5 to 8 pounds. They can be white with black, blue, chocolate, gold, gray, lilac, or tortoise. Their markings are extremely important and must be exact, always including a butterfly mark on the nose, colored ears, eye rings, a herringboned streak down their spine, a spot on the cheek, and a chain of spots along the body. Mismarkings are unacceptable in a show rabbit.

Harlequins

Harlequins originated in France in the late 19th century and are recognized for two very distinctive coat color patterns. The Japanese coat pattern has a golden-orange to golden-fawn base with markings in one variation of color. The Magpie has a white base with markings of one variation of color. With the checkerboard, banded, or barred look, Harlequins can have a coat that combines black and orange, blue and fawn, brown and orange, gray and fawn, black and white, blue and white, brown and white, and gray and white.

Their breed standard is very specific as to markings. One ear must be of a different color than the other. The face on the same side must contrast with the ear. The shoulder and feet should be opposite to this. The rear foot on the same side is the opposite color of the front foot, and a band of color must completely encircle the body. Any other coloring will severely penalize or disqualify the rabbit from the show ring. Their fur must be dense and sleek, either normal or rex textured.

"Harlies" are some of the larger mid-sized rabbits, weighing 7 to 8 pounds, and they have a variety of uses. Although they are excellent exhibition rabbits and devoted pets, they are also raised for their fur and for their meat as well. Although any rabbit has the potential to be gentle if he is handled enough and tamed correctly, the Harlequin has a reputation among breeders as being very laid-back and docile. They are also quite healthy, with no known hereditary health problems.

Lilac

As you'd guess, the Lilac rabbit got his name from his only acceptable color: lilac. They weigh between 5 to 8 pounds and have a very dense, thick, luxurious coat.

Rex

One of the most appealing of the medium breeds is the Rex, one of the older breeds of rabbits, discovered as a mutation among wild gray rabbits in France in the early 1920s. The breed's unique plush fur quickly made it a favorite among breeders and pet owners, and its popularity continues to grow almost a century later. Originally known as the Castorex

The Harlequin has a reputation among breeders as being very laid-back and friendly.

(which means "king of the beavers" due to the breed's unusual pelt), the two main characteristics of those early French rabbits–color and lack of guard hair–have been passed down through the generations as the quality of breed type has improved. Rexes come in a number of color varieties, including black, black otter, seal, white, broken colors, sable, red, opal, chocolate, castor, chinchilla, blue, and lynx. This is one of the healthier breeds, with no known genetic disease problems.

Rhinelander

Around the turn of the 20th century, the Rhinelander rabbit was developed as a separate breed in Germany. They weigh between 8 to $8\frac{1}{2}$ pounds. Sometimes called the "calico" of the rabbit world, the Rhinelander is one of the few true tri-colored rabbit breeds. They are marked much like a calico cat, with black and orange markings clearly apparent on a white body. Colored markings on the face, ears, and around the eyes give these little guys a very rakish appearance that most pet owners find endearing.

Rhinelanders are considered to be laid-back and gentle, and there are no known genetic disease problems known in the breed.

Silver Marten

The Silver Marten is slightly larger than the Lilac and English Spot, weighing between 6 and 9 pounds. Although the base coat can be black, blue, chocolate, or sable, each color must have silver-tipped guard hairs, which give the breed its name.

Living Large

If you can't keep up with a dog and don't want a cat, but like the idea of a somewhat large house pet, your eyes will most likely be drawn to the large breeds of rabbits. Some of them are truly an armful of love waiting to happen! Ranging from 9 to 11 pounds, there are plenty of breeds to choose from if you decide a big bunny is the one for you. Because of their size, these rabbits do have slightly different requirements than other bunnies, one of the most obvious being their housing requirements.

American

The American is one of the US's older breeds, with records placing it in America for more than 100 years. It comes in only two color varieties: blue or white. The blue variety has eyes almost the same color as the coat, while the white version has pink eyes. The American weighs between 8 and 12 pounds.

American Chinchilla

The American Chinchilla has a dense, fine coat that is smooth and glossy. Weighing between 9 and 12 pounds, he has a relatively round body.

Beveren

The Beveren is a large rabbit, weighing approximately 10 pounds. His thick, silky coat comes in white, blue, and black. Not commonly seen in the US until fairly recently, he has remained popular in Europe, where the breed was developed.

Californian

As you might expect from the name, the Californian rabbit originated in California. After a lengthy process of cross-breeding, the white rabbit with the dark-colored nose and ears that we recognize so readily today began breeding true to form in the mid 1920s. He looks similar to his cousin, the Himalayan, but he is much larger. This breed was developed for meat and pelt potential. They tend to be somewhat reserved but make excellent pets.

Champagne d'Argent

The coat of the Champagne d'Argent rabbit contains a rainbow mix of colored hairs that give him a silvery glow. He has been a very popular pet in the US, having come to the US from the Champagne province of France. The average Argent weighs approximately 10 pounds.

Cinnamon

Another rabbit that gets his name from his coloring is the Cinnamon. He only comes in a reddish-cinnamon color, with face, feet, and other points being slightly darker in color than the body. He weighs approximately 10 pounds.

Crème d'Argent

As the name implies, the Crème d'Argent was developed in France and is described as having a "smooth, silky coat of the palest orange." The average Crème d'Argent weighs between 9 and 11 pounds.

English Lop

There is no mistaking the English Lop, with his ridiculously long ears, which can be 24 to 26 inches long. This is a very playful, funny, affectionate, and intelligent breed and one that definitely requires daily personal attention. The fur is medium length and comes in colors ranging from chestnut, opal, lynx, black, and blue, to white, fawn, and steel. The English

The Californian is distinguished by white coloring, with a dark-colored nose and ears.

The average Champagne d'Argent rabbit is a popular pet, weighing approximately 10 lbs.

These six-week-old Cinnamon rabbits will eventually weigh around 10 lbs.

The English Lop is considered to be one of the oldest rabbit breeds in existence.

Lop is considered one of the oldest of the rabbit breeds, with origins in Algiers, North Africa, before becoming popular in Europe and the US.

Giant Angora

Unlike the other Angora breeds, the Giant Angora has only one color variety: White. He can have either blue or ruby eyes, however. Like the English Angora, he has hair on his ears, face, and legs. His coat is soft, with a fine undercoat (the actual wool that can be spun and woven) and straight, stiff guard hairs. He should weigh no less than $8\frac{1}{2}$ pounds.

Hotot

Also relatively new to the US, having been brought here from France in the 1970s, the Hotot weighs between 8 and 11 pounds and is distinguished by a frosty-white coat and a black circle around his eye.

New Zealand

New Zealands are a good choice for the first-time bunny buyer. Most well-bred New Zealands are outgoing, happy, sociable creatures that will enjoy being a part of your family.

This is a very healthy breed, with the exception of some eye problems related to their light sensitivity. They do tend to gain weight easily (they were developed primarily as a meat rabbit), so they must be kept on a stricter diet than some of the other breeds require. Although the white New Zealand seems to be what comes to the mind of most people when they hear the name, the first New Zealand rabbit was, in fact, red. They come in many colors now, all of them having a good, easy-to-care-for coat.

New Zealands are happy, sociable creatures that make great pets.

Palomino

As you might guess, the Palomino rabbit gets his name from his coloring, which is quite similar to that of the Palomino horse. Weighing about 9 pounds, the American-developed Palomino has an easygoing temperament that makes him an excellent choice as a pet. He comes in two color shades: golden and lynx.

Satin

The Satin was created here in the US and comes in ten color varieties, including black, Californian, chinchilla, chocolate, copper, red, Siamese, broken, white, and blue. As you might guess from the name, the coat of the Satin rabbit is indeed satiny-smooth and soft. His average weight is 9 pounds.

Silver Fox

Developed as a fur producer in Europe, the Silver Fox comes in both blue and black varieties, with hair measuring over an inch in length, with silvery tinges. The breed was originally known in the US as the American Heavyweight Silver.

As its name suggests, the coat of the Satin rabbit is satiny-smooth and soft.

Checkered Giant rabbits make great companions for busy families.

The French Lop is often referred to as the "bulldog of the rabbit world."

Giant Breeds

Even larger than the large breeds are the giant breeds. Giant breeds normally weigh at least 11 pounds, but they can weigh much more than that! Make sure you can meet the large housing requirements of these breeds before bringing one into your home.

Checkered Giant (American)

The American Checkered Giant is an energetic breed whose colors are limited, but the immense range of patterns in its coat makes up for the lack of diversity in color. The standard for this breed is very demanding as to color placement, with requirements including even eye circles, a spot on each cheek, two spots (or a grouping of spots) on each flank, and a central line going down the spine. These blue-and-white or black-and-white coated beauties are excellent choices for a very busy family, as they are so energetic they don't really require a lot of sitting and petting time. They do need to be handled daily from a very young age, however, although their temperament is described by most experts as very docile.

Flemish Giant (Patagonian)

Many breeders refer to the Flemish Giant breed as the "gentle giant" because of its gentle temperament in a body that can easily weigh from 13 to 16 pounds at adulthood (the largest of all the domestic breeds). Most breeders notice that their bucks are more playful than their does. They are available in black, light gray, sandy, fawn, steel gray, and white. This breed is prone to sore feet, so they can never be kept in a cage with a wire bottom, and they require adequate bedding to avoid injury. As with any of the giant breeds, arthritis (even in younger animals) is a concern.

French Lop

The French Lop has a big head with lots of loose skin that causes him to often be referred to as the "bulldog of the rabbit world." Because of the width of the head, some vets notice more of a problem with weepy eyes. Although chestnut agouti is the most common color for Frenchies, they can also be found in steel, opal, Siamese, blue, and tortoise shell, as well as the less common solid white.

Giant Chinchilla

The Giant Chinchilla breed is so named because of its coloration, reminiscent of a Chinchilla. One of the largest breeds, it tips the scales between 12 and 16 pounds.

With so many colors, sizes, and shapes, you're destined to find the perfect bunny for you!

Where to Get a Rabbit

You've done your homework, you've decided what you want from your new pet, and you know what breed you're looking for—now for the hard part: finding him!

Where will you find him? No matter where you search, some basic guidelines should apply. The rabbits should be housed in adequately sized cages, and they should be clean and have a well-stocked supply of clean water and food. There should be no overpowering stench of ammonia (urine) or fecal matter in the room where the bunnies are kept. There should not be a heavy smell of deodorizers that are being used to mask bad odors either. In ideal situations, the rabbits will have toys to play

Make sure the rabbit you may purchase has clean food and water.

Almost Perfect

Remember that an important part of being a responsible pet owner is to be able to accept and love a pet for all its qualities—both the good and bad. Make sure you are as prepared as possible for those bad qualities by always asking a potential seller of any rabbit you're interested in: "Why wouldn't I want this rabbit?" Then listen carefully to his or her answer and give it serious consideration when making your final choice.

Just as there is no perfect human, there is no perfect rabbit. Each and every one will have personality and behavioral quirks that will make him a challenge at times. Just be sure that those quirks are going to be things you can live with. Again, it's important to find someone that you trust so you can be sure that his or her answer to that question will be totally honest.

with and a selection of special treats. When you reach your hand into the cage, the rabbit may appear timid but should not frantically look for an escape, and under no circumstances should he appear aggressive to you.

Buying from Private Breeders

One option is to obtain your rabbit from a breeder. The advantage of buying from a private or hobbyist breeder is that the breeding that produced your pet has usually been carefully planned and thought through beforehand with regard to producing robust, healthy rabbits that meet their individual breed standards, including the temperament that is usual for that breed.

Because most breeders don't do commercial breedings of mass numbers of rabbits, they are usually careful to produce high-quality rabbits in every way. You will also have the opportunity to see the parents and know the date of birth of the rabbit you intend to purchase. Private and hobbyist breeders regularly handle their babies, so any rabbits they sell are used to being handled. This is a major benefit, especially if you choose a young adult rabbit instead of a baby. Buying from a breeder also means that you are getting a lifetime "hotline" for help with your rabbit. Responsible breeders want to make sure that the bunnies they send out into the world are happy in their new homes and that they're making their owners happy. They'll be more than happy to help you work through any problems, and they'll always want to hear success stories too!

Rabbit Rescue

To someone unaccustomed to the terms used in the animal world, the term "rabbit rescue" may bring to mind a red truck with lights flashing on its way to pluck a hapless rabbit from harm's way. While there is no red truck and no flashing lights, people who do rabbit rescue on a daily basis are no less "angels of mercy" than the paramedics, firemen, and other professionals who provide human rescue in emergency situations.

A Common Mandate for Rescue Groups

- To provide care for any and all unwanted, abandoned, and/or abused rabbits

- To rehabilitate abused, injured, or ill rabbits

- To find suitable permanent homes for all rabbits that are mentally and physically healthy enough to be adopted into new families

- To provide a permanent, safe, and healthy environment for the rabbits that cannot be rehabilitated enough to be able to exist in a family environment

Rabbit rescue groups work to find loving, permanent homes for homeless rabbits.

In this case, however, rescue refers to the taking in of a homeless animal that would otherwise turn up in a shelter, in yet another bad situation, or even worse, turned loose on the streets.

Unfortunately, while there isn't a 911 service for rabbits in need of rescue, there *is* a growing band of rabbit lovers joined into a network of rescue groups, whose sole aim is to turn unwanted bunnies into forever pets for lucky and deserving families. These guardian angels may be found at private or public shelters, and they deserve the undying gratitude of rabbit lovers everywhere for their selfless devotion to their cause. They work together in a nationwide network of fellow (unpaid) rabbit fanciers committed to finding good, loving, permanent homes for surrendered and abandoned rabbits. They also work tirelessly to educate the public on the proper care for pet rabbits. Each rescue group works with each other with the long-term goal of eliminating the need for any healthy rabbit to ever be euthanized because a forever home or foster home cannot be found for him.

Should You Adopt?

If you decide that you don't necessarily have to have a baby bunny, you should consider adopting an adult rabbit from a shelter or rabbit rescue organization. You can be assured that you are doing a very good deed, as thousands of unwanted rabbits are euthanized

Rescue organizations will ask potential owners many questions.

every year across the country because there are not enough good forever homes for them. Although some rabbits are placed in the rescue system due to health problems that their families found insurmountable (financially or emotionally), or behavior problems that their present owners wouldn't take the time to work through, the majority of these rabbits are homeless because of a lack of education on the part of their previous owners.

Too many times, rescue workers (of all breeds and species of animals) hear the same stories: "He was so cute when he was little, but then he grew up," "The kids don't have time for him anymore, and I didn't want him in the first place," "We are moving and will just get another pet when we get settled," " I had no idea they would shed so much hair," etc. Obviously, these people should have never had a pet in the first place, and one can only hope that they are screened more closely when they begin the search for their new pet, and that they receive proper education at that time regarding the serious responsibility of owning a pet.

Sometimes there are valid reasons for having to let a pet go to a new home. Sudden allergic reactions to the animal that do not respond to medications and treatments, unexpected job transfers, or other life-altering changes (including the illness or death of the owner) do occur to even the most responsible pet owners. In these cases, the owner usually works closely with rescue groups to find the perfect home for his or her pet.

If you decide to go through a rescue organization to find your new pet, be prepared to spend some time answering their questions. These questions will likely include the following:

• Describe what food you plan to feed and why.

• How will you choose your veterinarian?

• Describe your rabbit's cage and the accessories for it.

• Where will this cage be placed?

• How many hours a day will your rabbit be inside his cage? How many hours will he be allowed to roam outside of his cage?

• How will you rabbit-proof your home?

• What kinds of toys do you think are suitable for a rabbit?

Be sure you've done your homework before you attempt to adopt a rabbit from a responsible shelter. These people want to make absolutely certain that this rabbit, who has likely gone through a great deal of trauma in his short lifetime, is getting a forever home with someone who not only understands rabbits but is also willing to make the sacrifices necessary to be a good rabbit parent.

No matter where you decide to purchase your rabbit, just be sure that you know the upside as well as the downside to owning a rabbit. Also, make sure that you are committed to being his best friend, to creating an atmosphere where he can live happily and safely, and thus make certain that you are not going to add to the worsening problem of homeless and unwanted rabbits across the country. As long as your rabbit is well loved and you are in tune to his needs, there is no problem you can't work through together.

Just the Facts Ma'am

Don't be upset or insulted if you are grilled thoroughly by a rescue volunteer if you apply to adopt one of their fostered bunnies. These people are professionals, rabbit experts who want to be sure that they place the right rabbit in the right home. They want to make sure that the bunny is in a forever home this time and doesn't have to go through another major upheaval in his life.

They will screen you quite thoroughly about why you want a rabbit, what kind of home you can offer him, and whether or not you understand the responsibilities involved in owning a rabbit. Only after you have answered their questions to their satisfaction will they begin the steps to match you with the perfect pet. Don't be upset by their questions and their probing—remember, their rabbit charges are their first priority. Your wants and needs come second to making sure that the rabbit is safely ensconced in the perfect home for him (which works to your benefit, as certainly if he is happy you will be happy with him).

Cost

A rabbit adopted through a shelter or rescue facility will not be a freebie. There will be an adoption fee, which is not a "sale price," that will help to offset some of the costs involved with fostering the rabbit until he could find a home. Most rescue organization workers are unpaid volunteers, and running such an organization can be quite costly. In fact, once you have seen how tirelessly they work toward their goal of finding a forever home for every unwanted rabbit, you might decide to pad the adoption fee a little with a donation. (Many organizations have a non-profit status, and your donation would be tax-deductible.)

How to Adopt a Rabbit from a Rescue Group

First, find a rescue group and make an appointment to talk about the possibility of adopting a rabbit through their organization. Fill out whatever screening forms it requires, and answer any questions the group has for you. Be prepared to provide references from your veterinarian if you have owned pets in the past.

Once you have been approved as an adoptive parent, you should meet the foster parents, if possible, and learn all you can about any rabbit you are interested in. They can tell you their impression of each rabbit's personality and behavior, and you can better tell if he is suited to joining your family.

Before breeding your rabbits, ensure that the babies have forever homes.

Visit with your prospective rabbit in a quiet situation to make certain his personality will mesh with yours. Pay your adoption fee, agree to have your bunny spayed or neutered (if that has not already been done), and take your new bunny home!

Don't Be a Part of the Population Problem

It is important that you not add to the overwhelming numbers of pet rabbits in the US that are homeless and unwanted by producing litters of bunnies. Unless you have purchased a show-quality, pedigreed rabbit, have done your homework adequately, and are armed with facts to help you better the breed you have chosen by using selective and educated breeding practices, you should *not* breed your pet.

Pros and Cons of Adopting A Rescue Rabbit

The Pros:

- You're doing a good deed, offering your home and love to an unwanted bunny that may have had a rough start in life.
- You will have a veritable army of rabbit professionals to answer your questions about rabbits both before and after the adoption is complete.
- This rabbit will have likely been fostered and evaluated by someone who is a rabbit expert and can tell you exactly what to expect from this rabbit.
- You will be getting a rabbit that is likely already litter box trained, is past the juvenile chewing stage, has likely been spayed or neutered, and is exactly what he is always going to be. He won't get larger or change his personality.

The Cons:

- You may not get any kind of history (medical, temperament, feeding likes and dislikes, etc.) with the rabbit.
- You won't get to watch a cute little baby bunny grow into an adult.
- Your selection will not be as good as walking into a large pet store or visiting a breeder.

Why? One reason is that there aren't enough good permanent homes for all of the bunnies. Be sure that before you breed a litter, you have an adequate number of forever homes already ready and waiting. (And don't believe everyone who says, "Oh, I'd love to have one of Flopsy's babies if you breed her.") Make sure that potential pet owners are sincere and understand the responsibility involved in raising and owning a pet rabbit.

The only reason to breed a litter of rabbits is to try to improve the breed. You could actually do damage to the breed by producing below-average-quality rabbits that might have incorrect temperaments and coats, which will create a bad PR for the breed.

Be aware that the mother rabbit could die in childbirth. Not only will you lose your pet, but also you will be responsible for handfeeding a litter of baby rabbits, a daunting and disappointing task that will only add to the heartbreak of the situation. In addition, the babies could die, even in a healthy litter. Baby bunnies are frail, and the mortality rate for them is very high.

Education
Is the Key

Not only does a rabbit rescue organization or shelter offer a port in a storm to rabbits in need, but they are also an excellent resource for educating the public on the special needs of rabbits. They don't try to tell anyone that rabbits are the pet for everyone, but instead try to help each individual person decide if he or she is indeed a likely candidate for "planned rabbithood." Their websites are filled with educational information necessary for anyone hoping to open their heart and their home to a pet bunny.

Finally, it is expensive to breed rabbits. You can count on at least quadrupling the expenses you have now with your rabbit, not just doubling or tripling them. You will need extra cages, food, pans, dishes, and bottles, to say nothing of the extra veterinary bills for prenatal care for the mom and the postnatal care of the babies.

Shelter Wish List

Consider making a monetary donation or volunteering your services at one of your local rabbit shelters. Most of the time, rabbit shelters are run by individuals or families who pay all the bills out of their own pockets to care for the rabbits. Many go in debt to pay veterinary bills and supply store tabs. These people volunteer their time 24 hours a day, seven days a week to care for the rabbits in their custody. Even just a 10-dollar donation or a single bag of rabbit food can help feed several rabbits for a week. (Note: You can even purchase the rabbit food online and just ship it directly to the shelter if you choose to support a shelter that is outside your immediate area.)

Most shelters are also in need of old blankets, towels, food dishes, toys, etc. By volunteering your time or donating supplies or money, you can get not only a nice tax deduction (many shelters are registered as non-profit organizations) but also give your heart the warm glow that comes from knowing you helped make a lonely or sick rabbit's day a lot brighter. Working together, we *can* make a difference.

Pet Stores

Another resource for finding a rabbit is a pet shop. The selection at pet shops may be greater than through other available options, and many shops sell rabbits which may be either purebred or of indeterminate breed. There are good pet shops and bad pet shops, however, and it will be up to you to decide the difference. You should always insist on overall cleanliness in the surroundings, look for alert and healthy rabbits (and other pets in the shop), and insist upon intelligent answers to all of your questions from the staff.

You should discuss rabbit ownership with the pet shop employees and get as much information as possible from them.

Part 1

If the staff is knowledgeable, and the animals in the shop seem happy and healthy, you can feel comfortable purchasing your perfect rabbit at this establishment. It's best to get some kind of health guarantee from the shop though, ensuring that your rabbit is indeed healthy and without illness.

Also if you purchase from anyone who has large amounts of rabbits for sale, you should make sure that males and females have been housed separately, and the owners or pet store staff should be able to tell the sex of each rabbit they are selling.

Many owners purchase their rabbits at pet shops.

Purchasing "Second-Hand" Rabbits

Another option in purchasing a pet is to find a "second-hand" rabbit owned by someone who (for various reasons) has decided he or she can no longer keep the bunny. Although you may be able to find a fantastic bargain in a bunny with all necessary supplies at a very reduced price, be aware that if you're not careful, you can also purchase someone else's problems. Be sure to ask the owner about any temperament and health problems, and make sure you see how the rabbit is being housed and taken care of. Sometimes reasons beyond their control will necessitate someone having to let their rabbit go to a new home. Be sure the reasons are sound and are not concealing the real reason that could cause you heartbreak in the long term.

No matter where you purchase your rabbit, you should get some sort of guarantee as to his current health and what vaccinations (if any) he has been

Make sure the rabbit you purchase appears healthy.

Remember to keep the rabbit's best interests in mind.

given. If he has been to a veterinarian, you should receive a copy of all medical records as well. You should also receive some sort of bill of sale which includes not only the sale price, but also the age and sex of the rabbit and any known problems. Anyone who sells you a rabbit should agree to let you take him to the veterinarian of your choice to receive a full health checkup, and they should agree to fix any health problems that are found during that checkup.

It doesn't matter where you buy your rabbit. It only matters that you do your homework, be careful about whom you choose to do business with (even though you are purchasing a "family member," it is still a business transaction), and keep the best interests of you and the bunny in mind at all times.

Bringing Your New Rabbit Home

Before you bring home a new bunny, you should have everything well in place. This way, your new pet will have a happy home to settle into, where he can immediately begin to feel secure. If you bring your pet home and put him in one situation while you are working on fixing his permanent place, you will make your pet's homecoming a miserable time instead of a happy time, because he will have to continually adjust to different situations.

Just as you wouldn't consider bringing a new human baby home from the hospital without having first purchased a crib, blankets, formula, clothes, and all the other paraphernalia associated with babies, you should never bring a rabbit into

Set up all of your new rabbit's supplies before you bring him home.

Take your rabbit to a veterinarian within 72 hours of his arrival in your home.

your home until you know your home is going to be a safe, comfortable haven for him and you have gathered up all the paraphernalia necessary to provide for all his wants and needs.

First Things First

The first thing to do before you bring your rabbit home is to find a good veterinarian within easy driving distance of your home. Within 72 hours of arriving at your home, your rabbit should go in for a well-pet visit and exam and to complete the vaccination schedule that the breeder should have already begun.

But how should you find this vet?

• Talk to other rabbit owners; see what vet's name comes up most often with the most glowing recommendations.

• Ask a rabbit shelter volunteer.

• Let your fingers do the walking. Phone all the vets in your area and ask for their qualifications caring for rabbits or other exotic pets.

• Choose this vet carefully. Your pet's life is going to be in his or her hands many times during the years ahead.

• Make sure you feel comfortable talking to the veterinarian.

• See that the office personnel, as well as the vet techs, are friendly, knowledgeable, and seem to genuinely care about the animals. Ask to see the entire clinic and make sure that it is clean and orderly (taking into consideration how busy they are at the time and what types of procedures are being done).

Once you've decided on a regular vet, you should take these same measures to find a backup vet in case your vet is out of town or unavailable when you need him or her.

Where Will He Live?

You will need to buy a cage in which to house your rabbit when you are not home, when he will be unsupervised, or if you will be gone for an extended period of time. For better ventilation, his cage should be made of a wire mesh, with at least two levels. Aquariums are *never* acceptable housing for a rabbit, as they do not provide enough ventilation; a lack of ventilation will quickly make your rabbit sick and cause him to feel isolated, which will prompt him to exhibit behavioral problems.

You should also purchase a smaller carrying cage for vacations, day trips, or trips to the veterinarian. This cage should be kept equipped with its own water bottle, food dish, bedding, and litter pan, so that you will be ready for unexpected emergencies.

A Rose by Any Other Name

One of the most fun aspects of pet ownership is choosing a name. You may want to wait until you have lived with your rabbit for a few days before you choose a name, but it's always a good (and fun) idea to have some choices picked out ahead of time. Some rabbits will never learn their names well, so you don't have to worry quite as much about a name for their sake. Unlike dogs, which learn to come when their name is called, most rabbits will be more likely to come to a sound or a smell than a specific word, even if that word is their name.

Planned Rabbit-Hood

There are many things that your rabbit is going to need immediately, so it is best to purchase these things before the day that you plan to bring your rabbit home. The better prepared you are, the smoother everything will go, and the more comfortable your new rabbit will be. He will definitely pick up on your anxiety if you are scurrying around trying to prepare everything for him, and it will add to his already nervous psyche at being in a strange place with strange people.

The cage you purchase should have a solid floor to protect your rabbit's paws.

Storing Your Rabbit "Stuff"

Just like a human baby, one little rabbit will need more paraphernalia than you'd ever expect. From treats and toys to food bags and medicines, plus newspapers for beneath the cage and a myriad of other items, the area on top of his cage can soon start looking really messy. Purchase a good organizer tray to keep all the smaller items neat and tidy. Attach a few legal-sized paper holders (found in any office-supply store) to the side of his cage for keeping extra newspapers handy. Putting his food in a plastic canister with a tight-fitting lid will ensure that mice and bugs won't be attracted to it. It will also keep it from spilling, and you can keep the canister on top of the cage without your rabbit being able to chew through a bag.

Wood cages are not good choices because the rabbit is likely to destroy or damage them with teeth and nails, and the wood will absorb any "accidents," making these types of cages very difficult to clean.

What size cage you get depends on how much time the rabbit will be spending in the cage. If the rabbit will be out running around most of the time, a smaller cage will be sufficient.

Although wire cages provide very good ventilation, having a totally wire bottom is not acceptable. Wire mesh is hard on rabbit feet, so if you choose a cage with a wire bottom, you will need to cover a large portion of the floor area that isn't covered by the litter box and den with a piece of linoleum-covered plywood (or cardboard, although you should be prepared to pick up the pieces, as bunnies love to tear cardboard into pieces) to protect their paws. When purchasing a cage, check to make sure that it is sturdy and put together well. Also, check for sharp edges that are not filed down because these could hurt your rabbit. Make sure that you can reach into all parts of the cage for ease of cleaning as well as to get ahold of a frisky rabbit that wants to play.

Purchase a heavy, sturdy food dish that cannot be tipped over easily.

Food and Water Containers

Once you've decided on the proper cage, it's time to equip it. You will need to have a very heavy food dish for your rabbit. Plastic ones are not only easily tipped over, but they're very easily used as chew toys (which can be dangerous for your rabbit if the material is hard plastic that can crack and splinter). Crocks are excellent choices, especially if they can be attached somehow to the wire. Do not buy a small one just because you have a small rabbit. About 4 to 6 inches in diameter is about the right size for most breeds.

Drip bottles are great for dispensing water, though dishes work fine as well.

You can also check out the bird aisle for large bird food dishes that usually have a means of securely attaching to the side of the cage and are heavy and chew-proof as well. Most large animal-feed stores have rabbit supplies, and most will have rabbit feeders. These work really well if you have a pan beneath your rabbit's cage, as it will filter the fine dust from the food so it won't aggravate your bunny's nose.

Almost any size water bottle will do, but a 16 oz size is just about right. Most water bottles will have a small amount of leakage, so it is a good idea to either place a heavy ceramic

Shop Around

Shopping for your rabbit should take you into other aisles in the pet store besides just the small section reserved for designated rabbit supplies. Many food and water dishes that are designed for use in birdcages will work equally well for your rabbit, because they were designed for other critters that also like to chew and toss around their dishes!

Treats for hamsters and guinea pigs will be equally tasty to your rabbit. Cat toys are usually quite interesting to a rabbit as well (although be careful when making your choice—remember, rabbits are usually quite a bit more destructive than the average cat). When you're in a large department store, check out the baby section for indestructible toys, too. These usually have rattles and bells inside that will fascinate your rabbit.

dish underneath it or place the water bottle just over the edge of the litter area. Some of the newer bottles are easily filled without taking the bottle off the cage (the top pops up and then reseals) and they seem to be more leak-proof than other types. Some people use water dishes only, which may work fine for some rabbits, but the rabbits I've lived with have ended up either spilling the water or spilling food and litter into the dish. The drip bottle method seems to be more sanitary and easier to maintain.

Litter-ally Speaking

Anything that eats and drinks is also going to need a place to relieve himself. In the case of your house rabbit, that's a litter box. Look for a pan with sides at least 3 inches high all the way around. Having sides any lower means you'll likely have litter (and wastes) all over the floor. Small cat litter boxes work fine, as do plastic shoeboxes from a discount store (these also make excellent travel litter boxes, because they have a spill-proof lid) unless you have a standard or giant breed.

Obviously, the larger the breed of rabbit, the larger the litter box should be. Triangle litter boxes may work okay for some rabbits, although my own rabbits like to be able to put their whole body in the litter box when they are eliminating. The litter box will need to be secured in the cage, or you'll find your rabbit is likely to tip it over as he tries to burrow beneath it. Binder clips work well and so do bungee cords. Whatever you use, you will want something that you can easily remove but that the rabbit won't be tempted to play with.

Litter

Most regular cat litters are not good for rabbits. Clay litters are very dusty and can cause respiratory problems in rabbits. In addition, clumping clay litters have been known to clump up inside breathing passages and cause respiratory arrest. Wood shavings are not a good idea for rabbits either; in addition to being dusty, they may have aromatic oils that can cause respiratory problems in rabbits. Never use any kind of cedar chips with rabbits. Wood pellets, on the other hand, are excellent for rabbit litter. There are also some recycled newspaper pellets that have worked well for many rabbit owners. This is not only good for our environment, but is just as clean as the wood pellets and safer than clay litters.

Food

What you feed your rabbit, how much, and how often will determine his weight. Just like humans, rabbits come in all different sizes and body shapes. Rabbits sometimes gain more weight in the winter and then lose it again in the spring. Some rabbits just have a stockier build than others, which can make one appear heavier than another longer and leaner rabbit. When you run your hand down your rabbit's side, you should feel his muscles ripple a bit and be able to feel the ribs, but they shouldn't stick out or feel too bony. Little "love handles" are common in the winter. If he feels soft and "mushy" or looks pear-shaped, he might be overweight or just have poor muscle tone from insufficient exercise. Try letting him exercise more often and for longer periods of time, and try cutting back just a bit on his food.

Your rabbit will enjoy straw or soft fabric, like an old T-shirt, as bedding.

Bedding

Your rabbit will enjoy having some nice crunchy straw to bed down in. If you have placed some sort of den for him in his cage, you should put a few handfuls of straw in it for him. This can get a little messy as he tracks it in and out, so if you find you are having to pick up too much of it from outside the cage, try putting an old T-shirt or sweatshirt in his den to give him something to burrow into.

Treats

Treat time is a bonding time between you and your rabbit. There are many different types of treats that you can feed him; however, a good rule of thumb is if you are unsure if your rabbit can eat something, don't let him eat it. Baby rabbits have a very sensitive digestive system. You should never feed any fruits, vegetables, or other "wet" treats to rabbits under six months old, as this can cause diarrhea, which can be fatal. It is very important that you feed treats to your rabbit in moderation, as his basic diet should be pellets, which are designed for maximum nutrition for good health (discussed in-depth in a later chapter).

It is best to only give one or two treats a day at most. Some treats that are safe for rabbits of any age include: dry oatmeal (1 tablespoon), a tablespoon of whole grain cereal (mine seem to prefer Cheerios), one or two pieces of unfrosted shredded wheat cereal, one-fourth slice of bread (mine prefer whole wheat), or a club or saltine cracker. They also go

Acceptable Treats for Adult Rabbits
(more than 6 months of age)

- 1 tablespoon of dry oatmeal
- 1/4 slice bread (whole wheat is preferable)
- Unfrosted shredded mini-wheat cereal
- Unfrosted whole-wheat cereal (such as Cheerios)
- One or two club or saltine crackers
- 1/8 apple (don't peel it; they like the peelings, and they're healthy)
- 1-2 sections of orange
- 2-3 inches of carrot or celery stalk
- 2-3 inches of banana
- 1-2 florets of broccoli
- A few leaves of lettuce or cabbage (if you are certain they do not have pesticides on them)

Apples are great, healthy treats for rabbits.

into a feeding frenzy over empty ice cream cones, although that should be fed as a special treat because of the sugar content.

For rabbits more than six months of age, the selection of treats gets more interesting with the addition of a few fruits and vegetables. An eighth of an apple is a special treat, as are one or two orange sections or a couple of inches of a banana. Two or three inches of a nice juicy carrot or celery stalk is sure to get any rabbit's nose twitching, and a couple of broccoli florets can send them into paroxysms of delight. During the winter months, keep some grass seed on hand and plant a few pots of grass that you can keep in a sunny kitchen window. It's a nice addition to your kitchen décor, and your bunny will love to graze and keep it "mowed" for you.

Deterrents

Deterrents, such as Bitter Apple or Bitter Lime, can help keep a rabbit away from cords or anything else they may want to chew. Hot pepper sauce, alcohol, or grapefruit juice in a spray bottle may be used in extreme cases, too. (Some rabbits actually develop a taste for Bitter Apple, and this will actually encourage them to chew, instead of deter them.)

Toys

Many first-time rabbit owners are very surprised at how playful their rabbit is. Almost any rabbit will appreciate the addition of a few toys to his cage and exercise area. Their toys can be expensive and intricate or as simple as a cardboard box or an empty paper towel roll.

You can find many toys for your rabbit around the house, such as wicker baskets.

Toys aren't just for the rabbit's pleasure, however. You will find that a bunny that is kept amused with his toys will spend less time looking for mischief and new things to chew. A bored bunny will become destructive, depressed, and overweight. You should experiment to see what types of toys your rabbit seems to find entertaining, and keep rotating a good selection of those toys so that he always has something in his play area to keep him interested.

Be sure that the toys you provide for your bunny to keep him from getting into trouble don't provide their own trouble. If you see that your rabbit isn't just playing with some of his toys but is actually trying to eat them, switch to a different type of toy (e.g. from plastic to cardboard, cardboard to fabric, fabric to plastic, etc.) until you find a type that he enjoys playing with but doesn't see as a

> ### Toy Safety
>
> Be careful when you are choosing toys for your rabbits—soft rubber and latex toys are dangerous because your rabbit can chew off pieces and end up with life-threatening intestinal blockages.

potential treat. Be wary of giving him soft rubber toys or toys that have small parts that could be broken off and ingested. Rabbits are prone to intestinal blockages because their curious natures cause them to put things in their mouths that shouldn't be there.

You don't have to spend a lot of money to find playthings that your rabbit will enjoy. Be

Enjoyable Homemade Toys

You don't have to spend a lot of money on rabbit toys. Some of the things he will enjoy most are inexpensive or free, which gives you the added benefit of knowing you're "recycling." The following are safe and homemade toys that your rabbit will be sure to love.

- Paper bags
- Cardboard tubes from toilet paper and paper towel rolls
- Large PVC pipes (make sure they're the right size for your rabbit so he can't get stuck!)
- Willow wreaths (decorate with wooden blocks)
- Wooden blocks (be certain they are from untreated wood). Most cabinet shops will have a lot of interestingly shaped wood pieces in their garbage bin, free for the taking
- Branches from an apple tree (does double duty as a rabbit treat)
- Cardboard boxes (especially a closed box with two or three rabbit-sized entrance holes cut in the sides and filled with shredded newspaper)
- Untreated wicker baskets or other wicker items
- Wire cat balls (the kind with the bell inside)
- Hard, plastic baby toys such as rings, links, keys, rattles, etc.
- Parrot toys and bells
- Dried pinecones
- Towels
- Small, straw whiskbroom
- Straw hamster houses filled with timothy hay or alfalfa
- Stuffed animals (be sure they don't have eyes, etc. that can be chewed off and swallowed)
- Large rubber ball
- Box full of shredded paper (preferably ink-free)

creative and think of things you have lying around the house that your bunny could put to good use.

Rabbit-Proofing Your Home

Before you let your new rabbit run loose around your house, you will need to rabbit-proof it. Rabbits are curious creatures and can easily find their way into places you never thought they could go. Remember, in their natural habitat, they are burrowers. They were bred to

Variety Is the Spice of Life

Rabbits like variety; they get bored easily. Alternate any toys you give them so they always have something "new" to play with. If they haven't seen a toy in several days, they'll react as if they've never seen it before. (Hey, rabbits are cute, but nobody said they had long attention spans!)

Bunny Wreaths

An unpeeled willow wreath decorated with three soft-chew wood blocks and one hardwood decoration is a great toy for your rabbit. Not only is this wreath fun to tear apart, but it's also good for the teeth (all that chewing!) and the GI tract. (Most bunnies ingest the entire willow wreath! Extra fiber!) It also has aesthetic value, being cute and decorative. Attach it to your cage and let your bunny "redecorate," or just leave it on the floor for him to fling and chew.

dig their way into the ground to make their homes. If they find their head will fit, their body will soon follow.

To be sure that you've thought of everything, you will need to crawl around your entire house on your hands and knees looking for small holes, crevices, loose ventilation covers, etc. Even if your rabbit will be confined to certain rooms, sooner or later, he will slip past the barriers and get into "off-limits" areas, and it is better to be prepared for this event so you don't have to panic, wondering if he's trapped somewhere, or worse yet, loose outdoors.

You will need to check over all appliances for holes and areas that the rabbit could get inside, especially refrigerators, because some of them are designed so that a rabbit could get inside the back and hurt himself on the fan.

Never underestimate the ability of a rabbit to get into trouble in a place that you thought was safe. Rabbit-

Because rabbits are curious creatures, you will need to "rabbit-proof" your home.

Keep your rabbit safe from the springs in beds, couches, and recliners.

proofing is not something that is done once and then forgotten about. It is a constant endeavor to stay one step ahead of these furry mischief-makers.

Kitchen and Bathroom Cabinets

There is usually a gap inside kitchen and bathroom cabinets that your rabbits could easily get into, and there could even be an opening into the wall that you are not aware of. Make sure to close off any of these gaps or openings.

Beds, Couches, and Recliners

A box spring, couch, or any other furniture that has springs is an accident waiting to happen for a rabbit. An easy way to combat this problem is to staple a sheet (pulled tight), a plastic carpet protector, or a piece of plywood to the bottom of your furniture. Recliners and sofa beds are great to have, but if you're going to own a rabbit, you really should modify the furniture, get rid of it, or be *extremely* careful! A rabbit can get caught in the moving wires, clamps, etc., without you realizing it, with tragic results.

Electric Wires, Computer Cords, and Phone Cords

Rabbits are prone to chew on wires, a habit that is obviously quite dangerous. To help avoid this situation, you can pull all the wires together and through a plastic wire protector (or other tubing). If that fails, or if it's impossible to do for some reason, just be sure you have pulled the wires up out of view of the rabbit, and supervise him when he is in a room with unprotected wiring.

Open Railings

If you live in a multi-level home and your rabbits are allowed full access, open stair or balcony railings can present a big hazard to your pet, as he may decide he is related to a flying squirrel and take a flying leap into the wild blue yonder. You can either restrict your rabbit only to the lower level of your home with a gate or other blocking device, or you can purchase Plexiglas sheets or hardware cloth to intertwine between the spindles to protect your rabbit from going/falling through.

Poisons

A lot of things that might not be poisonous to humans can have a deadly effect on our rabbits. Something as seemingly innocent as a bowl of potpourri or a cigarette butt in an ashtray can mean death to an inquisitive rabbit. Be sure that all chemicals are behind a locked (and well-sealed) door, and that all potentially harmful houseplants are up out of their reach.

Antifreeze

This substance contains ethylene glycol, has a sweet taste that attracts animals, and is deadly even in small doses. What can you do to avoid it? Put "safe" antifreeze in your car this winter, one that contains propylene glycol, which is safe if ingested only in small amounts.

Pesticides

Many pesticides that we think are safe because they are used in over-the-counter flea- and tick-control products may be toxic to some companion animals. Never use any over-the-counter product on your rabbit without clearing it first with your rabbit-savvy veterinarian.

Fertilizer and Plant Food

Fertilizer and plant food seem harmless enough, but either can be fatal if ingested by your bunny. Make sure your bunny is never on your lawn unsupervised and alone.

Human (Adult or Children) Prescription Drugs

Human medicines, including over-the-counter products, can be very toxic to your rabbit. Unless your veterinarian has approved their use on rabbits, keep your medications to yourself and away from your rabbit.

Choking Hazards

There are many common household items that you might not consider to be potentially dangerous to your rabbit, but they may actually be choking hazards. Some of these are: the buttons on your remote control, toys that can splinter into pieces if chewed, Styrofoam packing, peanuts, pencil erasers, earrings, children's plastic building blocks, etc. Intestinal blockages are extremely common for rabbits, as they will put anything in their mouths that appears interesting to them.

Untreated lawns are usually safe for rabbits.

Part 1

Part 1

Appliances

Check under or behind the refrigerator, oven, washer, dishwashers, etc. to be sure that there is no way for a rabbit to get inside the appliance even when it is closed. Before running your dishwasher, always check inside thoroughly and make sure no rabbit hopped his way in when you weren't looking.

Plants Poisonous to Rabbits

The following plants listed are known to be toxic to rabbits, so when you are rabbit-proofing your home, make sure your rabbit will not have access to any of these plants. (The parts of the plants to avoid are included in parentheses.)

Agave (leaves)

Almond

Aloe

Amaryllis (bulbs)

Andromeda

Anemone

Angel's Trumpet

Apple (seeds)

Apricot (all parts except fruit)

Asian Lily

Asparagus Fern

Australian Nut

Make sure that the plants your rabbit can access are non-toxic.

Autumn Crocus

Avocado

Balsam Pear (seeds, outer rind of fruit)

Baneberry (berries, roots)

Barbados Lily

Begonia

Betel-nut Palm

Bird of Paradise (seeds)

Bitter Cherry (seeds)

Bittersweet (American & European)

Black Nightshade

Black Walnut (hulls)

Bloodroot

Bluebonnet

Boston Ivy

Buddhist Pine

Busy Lizzie

Buttercup (leaves)

Black Locust
(seeds, bark, sprouts, foliage)

Blue-green Algae (some forms toxic)

Bloodroot

Boxwood (leaves, twigs)

Bracken Fern

Branching Ivy

Buckeye (seeds)

Buckthorn (berries, fruit, bark)

Apples are great treats for rabbits, but the seeds can be toxic.

Part 1

Bull Nettle

Buttercup (sap, bulbs)

Cactus Thorn

Caladium

Calendula

Calico Bush

Calla Lily (rhizome, leaves)

Caladiur (leaves)

Carnation

Carolina Jessamine

Castor Bean (seed, leaves, oil)

Celastrus

Ceriman

Chalice Vine (all parts)

Cherry Tree (bark, twig, leaves, pits)

China Coll

Chinaberry Tree

Chinese Bellflower

Chinese Lantern

Chinese Evergreen

Choke Cherry (seeds)

Christmas Candle (sap)

Christmas Rose

Chrysanthemum Cineraria

Clematis

Climbing Nightshade

Coffee Bean

Plant food and fertilizer are toxic to rabbits, so make sure your pet doesn't ingest treated plants.

Cone Flower

Coral Plant (seeds)

Cordatum

Corn Plant

Cowbane

Cowslip

Crown of Thorns

Cuban Laurel

Cuckoopint (all parts)

Cutleaf Philodendron

Cycads

Cyclamen

Daffodil (bulbs)

Daisy

Daphne (berries, bark)

Datura aka "trumpet flower" (berries)

Day Lily

Deadly Amanita (all parts)

Deadly Nightshade

Death Camas (all parts)

Delphinium (all parts)

Devil's Ivy

Dieffenbachia (leaves)

Dogbane

Dracaena

Part 1

Daffodil flowers are not harmful, but their bulbs are toxic to rabbits.

Dumb Cane

Dutchman's Breeches

Easter Lily

Eggplant (all but fruit)

Elderberry (unripe berries, roots, stems)

Elephant Ear (leaves, stem)

Emerald Feather

English Laurel

English Ivy (berries, leaves)

Eucalyptus

False Hellebore

False Henbane (all parts)

False Parsley

Fiddle Leaf Fig

Fireweed

Flamingo Plant

Florida Beauty

Flowering Maple

Flowering Tobacco

Foxglove (leaves, seeds)

Garden Sorrel

Geranium

German Ivy

Ghostweed (all parts)

Giant Touch-me-not

Many flowers are safe even though their seeds or leaves are toxic.

Glacier Ivy

Gladiola

Glory Lily

Gold Dust

Golden Chain (all parts)

Golden Pothos

Green Gold

Hahn's Ivy

Hart Ivy

Hawaiian Ti

Heartleaf Philodendron

Heavenly Bamboo

Hemlock, Poison (all parts)

Hemlock, Water (all parts)

Henbane (seeds)

Hogwart

Holly (berries)

Horse Chestnut (nuts, twigs)

Horsehead Philodendron

Horsetail Reed

Hurricane Plant

Hyacinth (bulbs)

Hydrangea Impatiens

Indian Hemp

Indian Rubber

Indian Turnip (all parts)

Indigo

Monitor your rabbit when he is outdoors in case toxic plants are nearby.

Inkberry

Iris (bulbs)

Ivy, Boston & English (berries, leaves)

Jack-in-the-Pulpit (all parts)

Japanese Euonymus

Japanese Show Lily

Japanese Yew

Jasmine

Java Bean (uncooked bean)

Jerusalem Cherry (berries)

Jessamine

Jimson Weed (leaves, seeds)

Johnson Grass

Jonquil

Juniper (needles, stems, berries)

Laburnum (all parts)

Lace Fern

Lacy Tree Philodendron

Lady Slipper

Lantana (immature berries)

Larkspur (all parts)

Laurel (all parts)

Laurel Cherry

Lily of the Valley (all parts)

Lima Bean (uncooked bean)

Lobelia (all parts)

Locoweed (all parts)

Lords and Ladies (all parts)

Lupine

Macadamia Nut

Madagascar Dragon Tree

Manchineel Tree

Marbel Queen

Marsh Marigold

Mauna Loa Peace Lily

Mayapple (all parts except fruit)

Meadow Saffron

Medicine Plant

Mesquite

Mexican Breadfruit

Mescal Bean (seeds)

Milk Bush

Milkweed

Mistletoe (berries)

Mock Orange (fruit)

Monkshood (leaves, roots)

Moonflower

Morning Glory (all parts)

Mother-in-law

Mountain Laurel

Mushrooms
(some, best to not feed any, just in case)

Mustard (root)

Nandina

Narcissus (bulbs)

Needlepoint Ivy

Nephytis

Nicotiana

Nightshades (berries, leaves)

Nutmeg

Oak (acorns, foliage)

Oleander (leaves, branches, nectar)

Oxalis

Though some plants may look appetizing to your rabbit, they may not be safe.

Panda	Pokeweed
Parlor Ivy	Poppy
Parsnip	Potato (eyes and new shoots, green parts)
Patience Plant	Precatory Bean
Peace Lily	Primrose
Peach (leaves, twigs, seeds)	Primula
Pear (seeds)	Privet (all parts)
Pencil Cactus	Purple Thornapple
Peony	Queensland Nut
Periwinkle	Ranunculus
Peyote	Red Emerald
Philodendron (leaves, stem)	Red Lily
Plum (seeds)	Red Princess
Plumosa Fern	Rhododendron (all parts)
Poinsettia (leaves, flowers)	Rhubarb (leaves)
Poison Ivy	Ribbon Plant
Poison Oak	Ripple Ivy
Poison Sumac	Rosary Pea (seeds)

Rubrum Lily

Sago Palm Schefflera

Self-branching Ivy

Sennabean

Shamrock Plant

Silver Pothos

Skunk Cabbage (all parts)

Snake Palm

Snowdrop (all parts)

Solomon's Seal

Spindleberry

Split Leaf Philodendron

Star of Bethlehem

Stinkweed

String of Pearls

Sweet Pea (seeds and fruit)

Tansy

Taro Vine

Thornapple

Tiger Lily

Toadstools

Tobacco (leaves)

Tomato (leaves, vines)

Tree Philodendron

Tulip (bulb)

Umbrella Plant

Vinca

Most vegetables, such as carrots, are healthy and safe for your rabbit.

Violet (seeds)

Virginia Creeper (berries, sap)

Walnuts (hulls, green shells)

Weeping Fig

Western Lily

Wild Carrots

Wild Cucumber

Wild Parsnip

Wild Peas

Wisteria (all parts)

Wood Lily

Wood-rose

Yam Bean (roots, immature pods)

Yellow Jasmine

Yew (needles, seeds, berries)

Yucca

New Carpet

If you put down new carpet in your home, you should wait until the "newness" has worn off before you let your rabbit on it. The dyes can irritate his sensitive nasal lining, and in severe cases, can irritate his tender feet as well. If your rabbit is going to be spending a lot of time loose in your carpeted rooms, you should be sure his toenails are kept trimmed very short, especially if your carpet is a Berber or other looped pattern material.

Cage Safety

Many pet owners think that because they purchased a rabbit cage from a well-known pet supply manufacturer and paid full retail price for it, it will be totally safe for a bunny. Unfortunately, if there's a way a bunny can get into trouble, he probably will.

If your cage has a wire floor, you should cover most of it with linoleum, carpet scrap (not new carpet, as the dyes can be offensive to a rabbit's sensitive nasal passages), or newspaper. (If you use newspaper, your rabbit will consider it part of his entertainment–not for reading but for shredding!) Having a rabbit on a total-wire floor is asking for problems, as it can lead to sore feet and hocks, as well as cause him to get a toe or toenail caught in the wire squares, with painful consequences.

You should also be sure that there are no sharp edges protruding from the places where the wire sides, top, and bottom were fastened to each other. Many times, wires will have burrs that can rip a rabbit's tender skin.

If your cage has a door that opens down to become a "ramp" for going in and out, make sure it is sturdy enough for your rabbit. Many rabbit manufacturers don't seem to take into consideration the fact that some of the rabbits that will be prancing around in their cages can weigh over 15 pounds. Be sure any ramp or walkway (inside or outside the cage) can support your rabbit's adult weight.

Your Rabbit's Adjustment to His New Home

The great day has arrived. You didn't have to go to the hospital maternity ward and endure labor pains, but you have a new baby just the same. Just as you would have done for a human baby, you have the "nursery" all ready and all his supplies waiting for him. Anything that you think could make your new bunny happy is in place and ready for his attention.

His cage is placed where he can get attention without being in your way or overwhelmed with noise or activity. He has a comfortable den as his very own little bedroom inside his cage, and he has plenty of room to move around outside his den. He has food, fresh water, and nutritious, tasty snacks, including some timothy hay. He has

Make your rabbit as comfortable as possible when you first bring him home.

Walk a Mile In Your Bunny's Shoes

Put yourself in his bunny shoes for a moment, and remember what your new pet has probably gone through in the days leading up to this momentous occasion. If you purchased a baby bunny, he has only recently been separated from his mother and siblings for the first time in his life. He's homesick for the only home he ever knew. If you purchased him from a pet shop, you can't be sure what he went through in the days leading up to the time you brought him home, but you can bet that much of it was pretty terrifying through a bunny's eyes.

Imagine a noisy, bumpy plane or truck ride in a crate with a lot of other strange bunnies, all as terrified as you are, possibly being dealt with by people who don't understand bunny psyches and who don't offer any consideration for your feelings. Then imagine being stuck into a different cage in a bright, noisy building while a lot of strange, noisy humans walked around and looked at you or perhaps even poked and prodded or teased you when the store employees weren't looking. No wonder your bunny is going to sit back and take it easy while he figures out that nothing else bad is going to happen to him! Give him time to understand that he is finally in a place where someone loves him and understands him, where his happiness and safety is a top priority.

a batch of toys that the guy at the pet store told you his own bunnies went wild over. You also got some little wooden blocks for him to chew on, and you put them inside a little cardboard box he can use as a toy, too. His litter box is attached to the side of the cage so he can't tip it over, and it's got a layer of nice clean litter. Basically, he has everything a baby bunny could ever want or need!

But, wait—something's wrong. All he wants to do is sit in his nest and quiver his nose. When someone reaches for him, he runs to the back of his den and huddles. He isn't eating, he isn't drinking; he just sits there and looks around. Is he sick? Is he unhappy? Doesn't he like you? Will he always be like this? Like any new parent, you panic and reach for the phone to call someone and see what could possibly be the matter.

Letting Your Rabbit Make Himself at Home

Don't worry. It's natural behavior for a rabbit to sit back and take stock of everything when placed in a new situation. Let him set the pace for getting acquainted, and it won't take any time at all before his natural curiosity gets the better of him and he's out there rolling his rubber ball around or nibbling on his alfalfa bale and begging for your attention.

For the first few days the bunny is with you, it's vital that he not have any bad experiences. He should learn that his home is truly his "castle" and that when he's there, no harm shall befall him. Don't ever pull him out of his den, as that is the equivalent of your coming home and finding that your home has been burglarized. Everyone should have one place that is their safe haven, where they know they can go to be alone and unbothered.

Children should give the rabbit some quiet time so he can adjust to his surroundings.

If you have children in the house, it's very important for their future friendship with the bunny that they realize that until their new pet feels safe and secure, they are going to have to leave him alone and spend a minimum amount of *quiet* time around him until he gets used to them. It's important that the rabbit make the rules about how fast they get acquainted. Children must be patient and not follow their natural inclination to push themselves on the new bunny. If they want to spend time with him, give the child a book or quiet toy and have them sit in the rabbit's exercise area with him. They need to understand that, to the rabbit, they appear to be noisy giants, and they will have to prove themselves to him before he will trust them.

Think Like a Rabbit

When dealing with a new rabbit, it is important to be able to get inside his mind and think like him. Look around you. What do you see, hear, feel, and smell? Is the area in which you've placed his cage a draft-free spot? Is his cage so close to the TV or stereo that the cage bars rattle from the sounds? Will midday sun shine through that window on him? Is his cage so close to the window that the neighbor's dog can see him from your deck and taunt him? Is he near the spot where you enjoy sitting most often? Can he see you when you are relaxing? You know that your dog is just trying to make friends with the new bunny, but are you sure your bunny understands that? Try to think like a bunny, and you'll make his first days (and the years that follow) pleasurable and interesting for him.

Introducing Your New Rabbit to Your Other Rabbits

If you already own one or more rabbits and you are introducing a new rabbit into the family, you will face even more challenges in these important first few days. It's well worth the extra effort, however, for the years of enjoyment ahead.

Rabbits need other rabbits to satisfy their social and emotional needs. Unfortunately, because they are territorial creatures, you may face some dominance issues that exist between your current bunny and the newcomer. A worst-case scenario is that your original rabbit may attack the new rabbit with the intent to kill. At best, he may decide immediately that this new guy looks interesting and would make a great playmate, and he'll take the new bunny under his "wing" and show him the ropes. Because you can't be sure which scenario will take place, it's best to assume the worst and hope for the best.

Initial Introductions

Let your current pet out into an exercise area (preferably in a place that he doesn't consider "his"), and place the new rabbit in a secure place inside it. A folding dog exercise pen works great for this. Just put the new bunny in a small wire cage inside the pen so they can get to know each other through the wire.

Introductions are handled best when done on neutral ground.

Leave the rabbits alone to work things out among themselves. Unless you hear the sounds of battle and think that the new rabbit may be in danger of getting seriously stressed by an attack from the original rabbit (even though you know he can't do any bodily harm), just go about your normal routine. Don't give your original bunny any reason to think that this is a big deal to you or that it should be to him. The older bunny may show some territorial displays (such as thumping or jumping around, even over the new rabbit's cage, etc.) but most of the time, this is for display only and shouldn't pose any problem once the new bunny realizes he is safe in his little den.

It may take a few hours for the rabbits to decide that neither is any threat to the other. The new rabbit should start feeling more secure in his little, safe place, and the original rabbit will gradually start ignoring the interloper, presumably following the idea that "if I ignore him, he will go away." Once he realizes that the new rabbit isn't going anywhere, he will probably start allowing his curiosity to get the better of him, and he'll push his nose through the wire in a greeting to the new guy.

The First Encounter

After an hour or so with no signs of anything other than a natural curiosity and interest in each other and no aggressive displays, you can open the door to the new bunny's cage. Let him make the decision as to when it's time for that first encounter. Don't expect it to be a rapid decision. He may put his front feet out and zip back inside several times, "testing the water," so to speak, to be sure there is no danger. Keep an eye on them closely, but don't make any gestures toward either rabbit. This is a crucial time for them both, and it will make or break their future companionship abilities. Let them make friends on their own terms with no input from you.

Just as with humans, relationships between rabbits take time to grow.

Once the new rabbit has made the first venture into the other rabbit's space, there may be a few minor spats and scuffles. If the new rabbit has a safe place to retreat to, and the older rabbit doesn't follow him into his cage and continue to be aggressive, just leave them alone. They will have to come to terms with things on their own. Continue these introductions for a few days until you are sure the bunnies are getting along well together. Keep them apart for at least a week or so when you're not there to supervise. Remember, like any good relationship, bunny relationships take time to grow. Don't try to rush it or expect instant success.

The Importance of Spaying and Neutering

It should go without saying that you should never put two bunnies together that are not spayed or neutered unless you have a lot of names of people seriously interested in offering a forever home to the offspring. Unless you're seriously involved in breeding, willing to do

Reading the Signs

Once you've slowly introduced the rabbits to each other, you should be able to read their body language to see what to do next.

Love at First Sight

If you're lucky, the two rabbits won't have any squabbles during their initial introduction. If you introduce them in the space they're going to be sharing, and they still seem to like each other there, you've got a green light for the future!

Cautious Friendship

This is likely going to end well, but for now don't trust them alone together until you can be sure they can be trusted together.

Romantic Behavior

If a neutered male makes an attempt to breed with the female and the female doesn't seem to mind, this is a good sign that things are going to go very well. If she runs away from him, it will probably still work out okay–just take more time introducing them. If she becomes aggressive toward him, separate them and start introducing them very slowly.

Chasing

If one rabbit chases the other, this may just be their way of establishing dominance and deciding which rabbit is going to be making the rules. Just watch to be sure that the one being chased is not really being hurt and that he is not becoming too stressed from the aggressive behavior. Separate them after a while, and repeat the introduction until the chasing episodes either stop or become shorter in duration.

Actual Fighting

If the two rabbits actually fight, then you can prepare for a very long, very involved introduction period. Make sure that you put the two of them together in neutral territory (new to them both) for the times they are being introduced, and never leave them alone.

all the homework and legwork necessary (as well as foot all the extra bills) to breed rabbits successfully and correctly, have your pets spayed and neutered to make them more loveable, healthier pets!

Probable Scenarios

Although every rabbit is certainly different and you can never be certain about what is going to happen when he's introduced to a new rabbit or a new situation, most breeders find the following to be a good rule of thumb as to what to expect when you introduce one bunny to another.

Male to Female
(Both Spayed or Neutered)

This is the easiest combination to introduce. Put the female into the male's area to avoid territorial squabbles. Females will defend their territory to the death. Putting a male rabbit into a female rabbit's cage is tantamount to putting a mouse into a cat's bed.

If you plan to get two rabbits eventually, make sure your original rabbit is a male. It is much easier to introduce a female into a male's territory than the opposite.

Two Females

This is sometimes a good combination, especially if they are littermates. Expect some squabbles as they sort through their differences, but they should bond quite well eventually. You may see a few tiffs and squabbles among unspayed females during the summer months when their hormones are raging. (Another good argument for spaying!)

Two Males

This usually depends on how long it has been since they were neutered, whether they still have hormonal urges, etc. They'll usually fight at first but then end up tolerating each other. They'll rarely become best buddies.

Babies

Two babies of any sex will usually get along quite well; just be sure to spay/neuter early if one is male and one is female.

Baby and Adult Rabbit

This combination can be tricky, and the success of

Neutral Ground

Always introduce rabbits to each other in a totally neutral space, somewhere that neither has been before, so the older rabbit cannot feel territorial toward the new bunny. This can be a room your rabbit has never been in before, a safe enclosure inside your fenced yard, your vehicle, a sheet on top of your kitchen table, etc. Just make sure that your original rabbit won't feel a need to defend whatever you choose. If all goes well there, work up to introducing them in their living area and shared spaces.

Baby and adult rabbits can get along well if the older rabbit is willing.

the relationship depends on how tolerant the older rabbit is and how spoiled a family member he is. If he is the jealous type, this situation can be extremely volatile. Don't leave the two alone no matter how well they seem to get along until the younger rabbit is large enough to take care of himself in case squabbles occur.

Two Older Rabbits

If you purchase two older rabbits at the same time, they will quite likely bond as they explore their new space together, especially if they are the same sex.

Finding a Veterinarian

Finding a good veterinarian in the single most important thing you will ever do for your rabbit. No matter what kind of wonderful care your bunny receives on a day-to-day basis, everything can be lost if he is entrusted to the wrong veterinarian for his health care, especially emergency care.

It may seem like a lot of wasted effort at the time when you begin the search for what will become your family vet, but just remember that this person will most likely be responsible for your pet's life at some point. Think about how long you searched before you settled on the human doctor that became your family doctor. Doesn't your pet deserve that same consideration? An emergency

Finding a good veterinarian could be the most important thing you do for your rabbit.

How Do I Find a Veterinarian in MY Area?

There are an almost infinite number of ways to find a veterinarian (other than the Yellow Pages in the phonebook). Some of the best and most reliable include:

- Animal Shelters
- Pet Owners and Breeders
- Pet Stores
- Local Pet Groups (Kennel Clubs, etc.)
- Local and State Veterinary Associations
- Veterinary Schools
- Internet

The number for the American Veterinary Medical Association (AVMA) is: 847-925-8070. The AVMA can give you the numbers of state and local veterinary associations, as well as the names and numbers of various specialty groups and veterinary schools in the US.

is not the time to be flipping through the Yellow Pages looking frantically for help for your dying bunny. Take the time to do it right–choose your veterinarian when you have the time to relax and make informed and educated decisions, not decisions based on emotions and urgency.

Where to Begin

The first step in finding your rabbit's veterinarian is to try to get recommendations from reliable sources. Ask any local rabbit fanciers what veterinarians they use and recommend, question local rabbit rescue volunteers, and ask your local pet shop employees if they can recommend a vet for your rabbit. The American Veterinary Medical Association (AVMA) can also give you the numbers of state and local veterinary associations, as well as the names and numbers of veterinary schools in the US.

If these searches fail, do a search on the Internet to see if any vets in your area advertise their practice as one that includes "exotics" (which include reptiles, rodents, rabbits, and usually birds) or better yet, if they mention rabbits specifically. The House Rabbit Society's website (www.rabbit.org) has a list of recommended veterinarians. Hopefully, there will be one near you.

If you cannot get a recommendation, let your fingers do the walking through the Yellow Pages. Randomly select five veterinarians who do not advertise as avian or exotic specialists. Phone these veterinarians and ask them to whom they refer their rabbit cases. If the same name comes up five times, you have a clear winner. If not, phone another five and keep at it until you have one name that appears more often than the others. This should be the first veterinarian you check out in person. Keep the other names handy for follow-ups and as possible backup vets.

You should assume that any veterinarian who is not trained specifically in rabbit medicine will be responsible enough to refer you to another veterinarian who is trained in particular for exotic animals and rabbits. Also, with rabbits vying for third place as America's most popular pet, we can hope that veterinarian schools will begin to include rabbit medicine in their general curriculum. Until then, it's up to us as responsible rabbit owners to search out a veterinarian who has taken the time to receive education in rabbit medicine beyond what he or she needed to receive his or her DVM status.

Phone the veterinarian you have chosen and let the front office person know that you are concerned with finding the best possible medical care for your rabbit when necessary and that you would like to speak directly to the veterinarian either on the phone or in person when it is convenient.

Asking the Right Questions

You should have a list of screening questions ready for the vet when you talk to him or her. Try to avoid coming off as rude or a know-it-all, but do let the vet know that you are a concerned pet owner who wants the best for your rabbit and that you also do your research and want to know that your pet is receiving the best possible care.

How Many Rabbits Does the Vet See?

You should ask how many rabbits the veterinarian sees at the clinic each week. This answer may vary depending on the size of the town in which he or she practices, but you should never accept, "I don't have

You should ask the veterinarian how many rabbits he or she treats regularly.

Part 1

any rabbit clients now, but I do know how to treat them." You want to know that your bunny is in capable, qualified, and *experienced* hands! It's important to ask how many of those rabbits that he or she treats are house pets. Many people raise rabbits for their pelts or for meat, or they keep their "pet" in a hutch in the far part of their yard. For these people, the bottom line is likely to be about money and not emotions; make sure your veterinarian understands that this bunny is not livestock or a commodity but your companion, and you will always want the best possible medical attention for him.

What Kind of Anesthesia Is Used?

Once you know that the vet regularly treats rabbits, you should ask how many rabbits are spayed or neutered in the clinic and what type of anesthesia is used. The most common and much preferred anesthetic by most rabbit specialists is isoflurane. This is safe not only for the rabbit, but for the humans who have to be exposed to it. Methoxyflurane and halothane have been successfully used in rabbits in the past; however, they hold a higher risk of causing medical problems in humans who were exposed to it. In addition, methoxyflurane is dangerous to use on overweight rabbits.

Will Your Rabbit Need to Fast Before Surgery?

Another valid question to ask this potential vet is whether or not your pet will have to fast the night before his surgery. If he or she says yes, then it's time to question his or her abilities, as there is never a reason for a rabbit to fast. Rabbits do not have the same type of digestive system as dogs or cats; undigested food in a dog or cat can be aspirated into the lungs, causing severe problems during surgery. Rabbits, however, do not have this problem.

Rabbits do not need to fast before surgery, unlike most animals.

A good rabbit vet will also know that most of the "-cillin" antibiotics (penicillin, amoxycillin, etc.) cannot be used to treat infections in rabbits. He or she will assure you that rabbit medicine has come a long way since the days when rabbits were considered "fragile" and not good surgery candidates. Today's rabbits will have a lifespan almost twice that of rabbits a decade ago, because modern medicine is finally beginning to realize the importance of rabbits in our society, as well as their unique qualities and medical needs.

How Much Education Has the Vet Received?

It is well within your rights to ask the vet how much continuing education he or she has received in rabbit medicine. You'll know for sure that you've come to the right place if you find out that the veterinarian or veterinary technicians have rabbits of their own as pets. Ask how they prevent problems with their bunnies getting hairballs. If the veterinarian tells you that he or she gives them hay on a regular basis in addition to brushing regularly, you will know that you have found a true fellow rabbit lover!

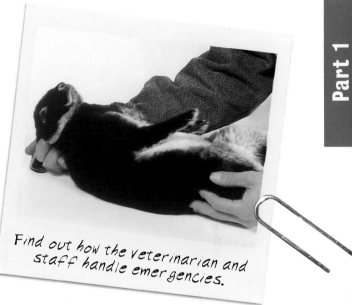

Find out how the veterinarian and staff handle emergencies.

How Does the Vet Handle Emergency Cases?

A very important question to ask the vet or his or her staff about is their handling of emergency cases. You don't want to assume that your vet will be there for you 24/7, only to find out that when an emergency arises, he or she doesn't take after-hours calls. In the case that the vet does not take emergency cases, ask the vet whom he or she refers, and make an appointment with that vet to ensure that this person, too, realizes you are serious about your pet's health care and want only the best possible medical attention when your rabbit needs it.

How Many Vets Are Available at the Clinic?

You should also ask (if there are multiple vets on staff at the clinic you have chosen) if there are other knowledgeable and experienced rabbit vets in the clinic who can treat your pet if your vet is not available. If not, ask to whom he or she refers in those cases, and check with that vet as well.

You should avoid choosing your veterinarian for the wrong reasons. A vet's proximity to your home is never a good reason for choosing someone. (Neither is choosing a veterinarian only because his or her prices are lower. Money is important, indeed, but not

The Question Checklist

Ask a veterinarian the following screening questions before designating that vet for your rabbit.

• How many rabbits do you see at your clinic each week?

• How many rabbits are spayed or neutered at your clinic each week? What type of anesthesia do you routinely use with rabbits?

• How much additional training have you received in rabbit medicine?

• Do you have rabbits of your own?

• What antibiotics would you suggest for a rabbit with an infection? (Most of the "-cillin" drugs, such as amoxicillin, penicillin, etc. are very dangerous for use in treating a rabbit.)

• What do you suggest as the best way to prevent hairballs? (A good answer would be "Provide your rabbit with hay on a regular basis, and brush away his dead hair frequently.")

• Ask if your rabbit can have food the night before his surgery. The answer should be yes. A rabbit's digestive system is different than that of a dog and cat; dogs and cats can have undigested food aspirate into the lungs, and therefore must be fasted before undergoing anesthesia. Rabbits should never fast.

as important as your pet's life!) Most dedicated pet owners drive by a dozen very good vets to get to the one they think is special. Giving your money to someone who doesn't know enough about rabbits is not only throwing away your money, but it can cost you the life of your pet. Don't chance it. Drive wherever it takes to get to the vet who you believe will do your pet the most good.

Part Two
Caring for Your Rabbit

"Wood chips are nice, but I'd rather have a good futon."

Housing

Although for many years rabbits were thought of as "outdoor animals" and forced to live lonely existences isolated at the back of the garden in wire-floored hutches, we now know that rabbits make just as good "indoor pets" as most cats, dogs, and other "usual" house pets. Furthermore, if you care enough to purchase a pet and make it part of your life, you should care enough to keep it close to you, and take the time to make it truly part of your family.

Even if an outdoor rabbit can avoid death from predators, poisonous plants, disease, bacteria, and parasites, what quality of life does he have? When a rabbit is cut off from human contact or contact with other rabbits, he receives no social

Rabbits are great house pets and are safest kept indoors.

Choose a cage that will serve as a safe, secure den for your rabbit.

interaction. In turn, most rabbits that live in an outdoor hutch will not be brought into your home and trotted out for your friends as a "pet." Left alone most of the time, most bunnies revert to being shy, timid creatures, their funny, sweet, gentle, and comical natures kept firmly under wraps with only the "flight or fight" mentality allowed to develop. It takes time to win the trust of a rabbit–it is not something accomplished overnight. Your rabbit must live in the house with you and share your usual sounds, smells, and activities before he will be comfortable with his family and let his true nature show.

Therefore, the cage you purchase will be one of the largest investments you'll make for your rabbit (except for medical bills in case of an emergency, of course). Cages come in all shapes, sizes, and types. Be sure you choose one that will be a safe and humane den for your bunny when he is not loose in the house with you.

Size It Up

Your first consideration is size. It's a given–bigger is better. Of course, bigger is also going to cost more and will take up more space, so you will have to take both aspects into consideration. The more time your rabbit will be outside his cage and loose in your house or exercise area, the smaller the cage can be. Don't think that by choosing a larger cage, though, that your rabbit won't need as much exercise time outside of it. There's no substitute for the social and mental exercise he will get from being loose with you, his best friend. All the toys in the world or all the tastiest snacks won't make up for keeping your rabbit shut away in his cage most of the time.

Most rabbit breeders say that a cage should be at least four times the size of a bunny, but few pet owners think this is enough room for their little fur buddy, especially when you take into consideration all the accessories you'll have inside the cage, as well as the rabbit himself. The House Rabbit Society suggests a cage no smaller than 36 inches wide by 24 inches deep and 18 to 24 inches high for average-sized breeds (5-10 pounds).

Get an enclosure that is large enough for him to have a space for food and water, a covered nest box that he can use as his "burrow," and exercise room. However, realize that no cage will provide enough exercise for an active, healthy rabbit, and he will still need an exercise area outside of the cage or to be allowed loose in your home on a regular basis. Allow more room in the cage for the amount of time the rabbit will be spending there.

Cage Floor

Although many rabbit cages have wire floors, consider how uncomfortable that is actually going to be for them because, unlike cats and dogs, they do not have pads on their feet, and their feet are very tender. The concept of having to put a rabbit on wire harks back to the time when all rabbits lived in hutches in the garden, their wastes going through a wire bottom to a mulch bed below where the kids could dig up fishing worms. This seemed appropriate at the time because it kept their litter from building up in the cage.

A cage should be at least four times the size of the rabbit.

However, because your bunny is going to be litter box trained, having a completely "drop-through" floor isn't going to be necessary. If you purchase a wire-bottom cage and then put a litter box in it, you will likely find your bunny sitting in his litter box

Rabbit Hideouts

Rabbits live in burrows deep in the ground in their natural habitat. Although our domesticated bunnies may prefer a soft fleece rug in place of dirt and pellets and tasty treats to grass and roots, they still have that innate desire to be surrounded at times by close, secure-feeling walls. Provide your bunny with a small, dark place inside his cage where he can cuddle when he needs some time alone. This can be anything you choose, from a cardboard box with bunny doors cut into it, to a professionally designed metal or wooden house. Just be sure that it is small, dark, and has some of your rabbit's favorite things (hay or other comfy bedding, chew toy, wooden block or treat) inside.

Part 2

Purchase a cage with a solid floor, or cover a wire-bottom floor.

most of the time, avoiding the discomfort of the wire floor on his tender feet. If your cage has a wire floor, place a piece of plywood or thick cardboard as a sitting area for your bunny.

You can find cages with slatted-bottom floors, which are more comfortable and still allow drainage for possible bathroom accidents and food and water spills. If you have already purchased a commercial rabbit cage that you realize now is not adequate for your bunny's needs, you can easily convert it into a wonderful home for your bunny. Just cut larger doors (be sure to edge the fresh cuts with the plastic spines from report covers to avoid scratching either you or your bunny), put plywood or cardboard over the wire floor, and place the cage on a dolly or other wheeled platform to make it easier to clean around.

Cage Location

Although a cage can be a place for security and quiet time, it is best to place the cage in an area of activity because bunnies love attention and can become lonely if isolated. Indeed, the placement of the cage is as important as what type of cage you choose. No matter how much you want your rabbit to be loose in your home, there will always be long periods of time when he will need to be in his cage for safety's sake (when you have company with small children or allergies to animals, when you're vacuuming or mopping or cleaning with strong chemicals, etc.) You want to make sure it is as pleasant as possible for him. A family room is usually an excellent place for his cage, unless your family is excessively noisy. In that case, you may have to work him up slowly to being able to understand and tolerate the noise.

Location, Location, Location

Ask any realtor what is the most important thing to consider when choosing a home, and they'll likely smile and quote, "Location, location, location." Ask an architect or home designer the same question, and they will tell you that the shape of your home and the rooms inside it, as well as the size and the location, affect the way you feel and the way you see life. Being in a place that makes you feel good is the reason you chose your home. Make sure that you choose a home for your bunny that will make him feel good; then put it in a place where he can feel like part of the family.

Although your bunny may have been chosen as a pet for your child, putting the rabbit's cage in your child's room usually isn't a good plan. Although most rabbits don't have a large vocal vocabulary and won't keep your child awake at night meowing, cooing, barking, or hissing, they do make noise. They are active at night (if you're a rabbit, being visible out in the open in the wild in broad daylight is equal to putting a large neon sign over your head that says "let me be your dinner please") and your child will likely be bothered by the rattles, bangs, and other noises coming from the bunny cage as his or her bunny eats, drinks, plays, and chews.

Place the cage in an area of activity where your rabbit will receive plenty of attention.

From the rabbit's point of view (remember, think like a rabbit!) a bedroom is too far away from the social activities going on in a normal house. Most active children spend very little time in their bedroom, and the rabbit can easily become neglected. You probably don't spend a lot of time in your child's room either, so the bunny may not be fed or watered or have his other daily chores taken care of.

Whichever room you decide to use as the primary "bunny room," be sure you place the cage in an area out of drafts and away from heater and air conditioning vents and duct outlets. Don't be tempted to tuck his cage away in an area where it "won't be in the way," such as the garage or basement. Would you want to spend all your time there? Neither would he.

Temperature

If possible, cages should be kept in the coolest and least humid area of the house, away from heat and drafts. Temperatures in the 60-70°F range are best for bunnies; temperatures in the upper 80s and beyond can potentially cause a fatal heat stroke. Rabbits can tolerate cold better than they can handle heat. Unless you keep your house especially cool during the summer, you might want to leave a bottle of frozen water in the cage and wet down the bunny's ears during hot weather to help keep him cool, calm, and collected. Also, marble or ceramic tiles may be used as a cool spot for bunnies to lie on in warm weather.

Part 2

Your rabbit's cage should have everything he wants and needs.

The Case Against Aquariums

When choosing a habitat for your new rabbit, do not select an aquarium or a solid-walled cage. These do not provide sufficient air circulation (which can lead to respiratory disease) and can also cause heat buildup in hot climates, which can quickly be fatal.

Accessories

Once you've got the cage located, it's time for the accessories. Your rabbit will see his cage as his "nest." Therefore, it should have everything he wants and needs to be truly comfortable. You should stock it with toys he enjoys (not all his toys at once–rotate them from day to day or week to week so that he always has something new to pique his interest) and tasty nutritional treats. A synthetic sheepskin rug will be greatly appreciated in a rabbit's nest box. Make sure the nest is enjoyable, and you will find he will enjoy being there, even when the cage door is open!

Why Not Outside?

No matter how wonderful his hutch or cage is, if it is outside, your rabbit is in danger. Even if the cage is predator-proof, after generations of being constantly preyed upon, your rabbit has developed above-average vision, hearing, and smell. A rabbit can sense the presence of a predator such as a raccoon, strange dog or cat, hawk, owl, or snake, even if the animal is not nearby or trying to get into his cage.

Many times, pet rabbits left outdoors overnight will be found dead the next morning in a perfectly secured cage, without a scratch or mark on them. What happened? He most likely panicked when a predator came close or tried to get into his cage, and he either

Danger, Danger!

Not only does a bunny face danger from predators if left out of doors (even in a "secure" area), he also faces other outdoor-related dangers:

- Pesticides
- Bacteria and diseases from other animals and insects
- Poisonous plants
- Theft, teasing, or torture by malicious humans
- Exposure to dangerous levels of heat and cold (as well as moisture and inclement weather)

If you want your bunny to get fresh air and sunshine, be a responsible pet owner and share it with him. When you go back indoors, make sure he comes with you.

injured himself fatally in that panic-stricken state or literally died of shock. Rabbits have very tricky nervous systems, and stress can easily kill them if it's severe enough. This might not happen only at nighttime, either. Your rabbit should never be left alone outdoors unsupervised, even in what you think are safe surroundings. The risk just isn't worth it.

Bedding

Choices for your rabbit's bedding may have to be made over time as you figure out your bunny's likes and dislikes. Cedar and pine shavings smell good and bring a "Christmasy" scent to the cage, but these should be avoided because their oils can cause health problems. Pine is safer than cedar (never use cedar under any circumstances), but aspen or spruce is a much better choice if they are available. Straw is always a good, safe bet when providing bedding for a bunny. It can also provide a late-night snack, as well as a mattress and pillow.

Fresh Air and Sunshine

Many owners allow their rabbits to spend time outside in an enclosed pen made from a wood frame with wire on all sides (including top and bottom). This allows the bunny to spend time outside and munch on the grass (provided it is not treated with any herbicides, pesticides, or other chemicals!) without burrowing out and with protection from unwanted visitors. You can move it from place to place in the yard, so he always has fresh, tender grass to nibble on.

Part 2

Many owners provide their rabbits with enclosed areas outside.

Shelter from sun, wind, rain, and other elements must also be provided, although you should never leave him outside in inclement weather. You should always supervise your bunny when he's outdoors, and always remember to bring him inside before dark.

Should He Be Loose In the House All the Time?

Although rabbits are thought to be nocturnal creatures, they are in fact "crepuscular," meaning that they sleep during the main hours of both day and night and are most active at dawn and dusk. If you want to make your rabbit truly happy, be sure that he is allowed out of his cage during those times of day. Otherwise, he probably should be safe in his cage when you are gone or do not have time to supervise him.

Moving In

Don't be upset if you move your bunny into his new cage and he immediately starts rearranging. Natural-born interior decorators, rabbits very rarely see things the way we

Bored Bunny

Even a rabbit that is given plenty of exercise and toys to play with can become bored. If he is in his cage and bored, probably the worst that can happen is that he will chew his wooden blocks a little more viciously, or he might learn how to thump the cage floor for attention.

If he is loose in your home and bored, however, your rabbit is an accident waiting to happen. A bored rabbit is often a very naughty rabbit and has the potential for getting into a lot of trouble, some of it possibly health threatening!

For instance, nosy bunnies on the prowl for something fun to do may find full ashtrays and become victims of nicotine poisoning. They can chew through electrical wires and electrocute themselves. If they think that the couch or recliner would make a good burrowing place, they can be injured by the folding mechanism or the springs if someone sits on the furniture while they are inside it. Give your bunny lots of fun things to play with and chew (boxes, baskets, vine and straw wreaths, grass mats, etc.) and be ready to supervise him the entire time he is loose in your home.

humans do. For that reason, anything that must remain in place in the rabbit's cage (water bottle, litter box, etc.) should be securely fastened. You will find that "securely" means something entirely different for rabbits than for humans, as many rabbits will persist with whatever catches their attention until they manage to unsnap, untie, or unfasten it. Don't be surprised if your rabbit gets busy immediately moving his nest box, food dish, toys, and bedding until he gets it perfectly arranged to his satisfaction, as seen through a bunny's eyes.

Cozy Home or Jail Cell?

As humans, we tend to view a cage as some sort of isolated prison, a place of punishment. A rabbit that lives his whole life in a cage may feel the same, but a rabbit that is allowed hours every day running free in the house with you will see it more as a den, refuge, or place of privacy. Never use the cage as punishment, but rather use it as an educational tool as you teach your rabbit the things he must know to coexist peacefully in your home.

In his cage, your rabbit will learn about litter boxes and toys while he has the freedom to do as he chooses without human supervision. You may decide that your rabbit is trustworthy enough to allow him access to your home all the time. In that case, don't put the cage out at your next yard sale, but instead keep it in case of illness, emergency, or company who can't be around your bunny. Who knows–you may become so enamored with your fur-footed friend that you decide to buy him a companion. You'll need that cage for the new rabbit's education as well.

Travel Cages

Not only do you need to purchase a cage for your rabbit's use while he is at home, but you should also

Make Sure It Fits

Keep in mind that if you purchase or build a cage that is wider than 24 inches, you may have problems getting it through some doorframes. Measure your doors before you begin building. If you want a cage that is larger than your door, consider building it in two pieces that attach together with snaps or hinges, or build a collapsible cage.

Part 2

Never use the cage as punishment. Your rabbit should see it as his cozy home.

Cage Tips

• Bungee cords and snap clips come in very handy for attaching bowls, boxes, and various bunny paraphernalia to the cage.

• Attach legal-sized letter holders (found at any office-supply company) to the outside of your rabbit's cage to hold extra newspapers (comes in handy for leaving notes for a bunny sitter, too)

• Purchase a nice-sized plastic box with a lid for keeping all your bunny supplies neatly in reach.

• If you use a dog exercise pen as a run or habitat for your rabbit, you can secure towels or a sheet across the top, not only for security but so your bunny will have more of a "den" feeling.

• It is important to keep your bunny habitat as clean as possible, but be wary of what chemicals you use for disinfecting and cleaning. Make sure that your products are safe for use around small pets.

• Never allow your rabbit to have rawhide chew toys. He would probably love them, but it is too easy for small pieces to get lodged in either his throat or stomach, causing serious health problems.

purchase a travel cage for him for fun travel, veterinary trips, and emergency trips. Travel cages also work well for "time-out" for a rambunctious bunny, isolating an ill bunny, as a den inside a larger cage, or even as a place to sleep for the bunny that is loose in a larger area. Using a travel cage this way is great because it will capture the pet's scent, and your bunny will always feel at home in it, no matter where he is. Be aware that he may enjoy chewing on it.

Most pet carriers are approved for airline travel, but if you plan to fly, check and make sure that the one you have is suitable. Only one size of carrier is approved for under-the-seat transportation; the rest must travel in cargo (not a pleasant ride for an animal!).

If your rabbit will be inside the carrier for any length of time at all, it will be necessary to include a small litter pan. Plastic shoeboxes are a good size for this and can be fastened to the carrier floor with heavy-duty, double-stick tape. Instead of litter, you might consider using baby or adult diapers to line the litter box or the entire carrier floor. A smaller drip-type container like the one they are used to on their "home cage" can be used for water.

Grooming

If you have chosen a rabbit with a "normal" coat, you will find that grooming is a breeze. Rabbits spend a lot of time grooming themselves and are very clean animals. If you have a breed such as an Angora, Jersey Wooly, or other breed with a higher-maintenance coat, however, you will have to budget more time for grooming, because it's a necessity for these breeds. All breeds of rabbit shed, so all bunnies should ideally be brushed at least twice a week, but longhaired rabbits will need it daily or at least every other day.

Bath Time

Rabbits are a lot like cats in their personal grooming practices. Rabbits use their paws and their

Most rabbits won't need much grooming because they groom themselves frequently.

Part 2

Your rabbit proba-
bly won't need a bath even
if he's been outside.

Making Fleas Flee

Fleas aren't just uncomfortable for your rabbit—they can quickly cause him to become anemic, a life-threatening condition. Therefore, use preventative measures to avoid the problem entirely before it begins. Advantage for kittens (obtained from your vet) can be used on most *adult* rabbits (for rabbits who are less than one year of age, consult your vet). Flea combs take more time but work just as well— without exposing your rabbit to potentially dangerous chemicals.

tongue to groom themselves on a regular basis, so with the exception of their getting into something sticky or dirty, you'll rarely (if ever) have to give them a bath. If your rabbit is part of a therapy program (hospital, nursing home, special education classrooms, etc.) there may be special requirements for baths, but on a regular basis, you'll find that your rabbit can take care of his own bath time.

If the situation should arise where you have to give your rabbit a bath, be sure that you follow one rule implicitly: Stop immediately if your bunny becomes frightened or overly stressed–rabbits can go into shock and die if their stress levels get too high. If you handle bath time in the correct manner, however, you'll soon turn bathing into something fun that your rabbit may even look forward to.

The Bath

Be sure you use lukewarm water. (Test it on your wrist, like you would a baby's milk bottle.) Run about 2-3 inches (deeper if you have a giant breed bunny) into the bathtub or sink. The rabbit may feel more secure in the sink or a smaller container. Remember, to him your bathtub is going to look like an ocean. You don't want him to be immersed in the water, but just have the water well up over his feet only.

If you don't have a good rubber bathmat to provide traction, place a folded towel on the bottom of the tub. If your rabbit feels secure, he will enjoy the session much more. One slip where his head goes under water (or makes him think it's going to) can damage his psyche to the point where he will never enjoy baths, and he will likely hold you to blame for his trauma as well.

Most people find that using a hand sprayer (handheld shower in the bathtub, dish sprayer in the sink) works better, although your rabbit may find the spray of the water uncomfortable and scary. If so, just use a plastic mug or other large container for dipping water and pouring over his back.

With one hand on the rabbit's back (for moral support, as well as physical restraint) use the other hand to gently swish the water around his feet and bottom. Every rabbit will react differently. Some will find the whole thing curious and exciting; others will be sure that it's torture, and they'll fight it tooth and toenail (literally).

Lightly scoop water along the areas to be washed, keeping water away from the face and ears. Unless you're dealing with something particularly smelly, sticky, or otherwise distasteful on their coat, most people find that a simple water bath is sufficient to clean the coat. However, for tougher cases, you can use a shampoo specially formulated for rabbits. Never use any flea and tick shampoos on your bunny, as some are potentially dangerous, even fatal.

Once your bunny is well lathered, use the method above to scoop water over him, rinsing as much soap as possible from his fur. For the final rinse, you should use either the hand sprayer, or you can drain the tub and refill with fresh water. (Be aware that the sound of a drain gurgling is very distasteful and scary to most rabbits.)

Drying Your Rabbit

Although you can't actually wring out your bunny, you should use your hands like a "squeegee" to get as much excess water as possible from his fur before putting a dry towel around him. Make sure that it is warm in the area where you plan to dry your bunny. Being wet is uncomfortable enough for him; adding a chill will not only be unpleasant for him but can also lead to illness. Rabbits will quickly lose body heat if they are left wet and cold for any length of time. Most rabbits will tolerate a good rubdown with the towel to blot most of the excess water. Many can even be trained to be dried with a hair dryer–just make sure it's on the lowest setting of both heat and air force.

When deciding if the rabbit is dry, don't just feel the outer fur, but run your fingers clear to the skin to be sure that they are totally dried. Angoras, Jersey Woolys, Rex rabbits, or any breed with a dense or plush coat will take much longer to dry. You should also be sure that the areas in the folds of skin are dry as well, especially the folds of the dewlaps, the base of the tail, and between the legs.

Brushing and Combing

Grooming any breed of rabbit includes brushing and combing. Even rabbits with normal, short, or plush coats will benefit from regular brushing and stroking with a grooming glove. This regular grooming brings down the natural oils from the base of each hair and down the shaft, providing a healthy sheen and natural protection from the elements. Grooming time isn't just for beauty and bonding with your pet—it is a very good time to get to know your rabbit's body and learn what changes might be indicative of health concerns.

The time you spend brushing your rabbit can be a pleasant experience for you both if you do it correctly. First, be sure you don't brush too aggressively. Bunny skin is very tender and delicate and can easily tear if you use a brush that has bristles that are too stiff or if you brush too hard. Even if your bunny has short or plush hair, you'll find that brushing him routinely will eliminate a lot of excess hair floating around your home, and it will also greatly reduce the chance of hairball impactions that are likely to occur if your pet grooms himself and swallows the dead hair. Most rabbits don't like their hair to be brushed "against the grain" (not in the direction it grows), so they will usually struggle to get away. Just remember, brush gently, using a soft brush, and brush in the direction that hair grows, being sure to reach completely to the skin without actually putting pressure on the skin. Don't be surprised if your rabbit runs toward you when he sees the brush, almost as fast as he runs for a carrot.

All rabbit breeds should be brushed and combed regularly.

Brush your rabbit gently in the direction the fur grows.

While you're brushing, combing, and doing nails, always feel your bunny carefully from head to toe (including the feet, nails, and teeth), parting the hair and checking for lumps, bumps, cuts, wounds, or fleas, as well as keeping an eye out for overgrown nails, teeth, or any other changes or possible or potential health problems. Although most rabbit owners find that using a dog grooming table makes grooming time easier, you may find that you get by quite nicely grooming your bunny with just a towel spread across your lap while you're watching TV or by putting a rubber bathmat on top of a high table or clothes washer or dryer. Never leave him unattended on anything high, however. Although some people will tell you that rabbits won't jump from heights, no one explained that to my fearless bunnies.

Ear Care

Besides being the cutest part of any rabbit, the ears are one of the most important parts on which to maintain good grooming practices. You should check your rabbit's ears every time you brush him. There should never be any odor, redness, or swelling. If you see a waxy buildup in the outer canal, you can use a cotton swab dipped in a mild solution of vinegar and water to remove it, but be careful not to push it deeper into the canal. *Never* put anything into the deep part of the ear canal.

Ears with any sign of pus or infection are a reason to go to your vet immediately. Scaly ears that your bunny seems to rub or scratch a lot are a signal of ear mites, a condition that also should be treated by your veterinarian. Most over-the-counter medications only exacerbate the situation.

Nail Trimming

Even if your rabbit learns to tolerate nail clipping, it is never a truly pleasurable experience for him. Make sure you make the session as pleasant as possible by using nail clippers designed for small animals. Although human nail clippers can be used, they are usually not sharp enough for a swift, clean cut and may crush or pinch the nail.

Grooming Tools

Before your bunny is ready for his first grooming, make sure you have the correct tools on hand.

√ Soft-bristled brush (some breeds require a slicker brush to do an adequate job, but be sure you get the most gentle one available…regular dog slicker brushes will tear a rabbit's tender skin)

√ Flea comb

√ Toenail clippers

√ Styptic pencil

√ Nail trimmers

√ Cotton swabs

√ Mat splitter or mat rake (for longhaired breeds)

Part 2

Trim only the tip of the nail in a firm, swift motion.

What to Do If the "Quick" Is Cut

Although the sight of blood is always time to panic for pet owners, don't worry if you cut a toenail too short. It happens to us all. Even rabbit professionals will occasionally cut into the quick of the nail and have to reach for the styptic powder. If you don't have the right product on hand if this occurs, don't panic. Just put a pinch of flour or cornstarch on the nail or gently place the nail in a softened bar of soap.

Before your nail-trimming session starts, gather all your necessary equipment. This includes small-animal nail trimmers, a towel, cotton swabs, styptic pencil or other blood-clotting agent, and hopefully someone to help you. Wrap the bunny in the towel to keep him from hurting himself or you during the trimming. Be sure you trim only the tip of the nail. The flesh of a rabbit's toe extends inside the toenail, an area known as the "quick." Cutting into this flesh will cause him to bleed and can create a problem with infection if it's not treated correctly. Take off only the tip and trim frequently to keep the quick from growing out into the nail.

Place the clippers on the nail where you want the cut to be. Apply gentle pressure and cut in a firm, swift motion to avoid crushing the toenail instead of producing a clean cut. If you see a drop of blood, quickly apply a blood-clotting agent to the tip of the nail. There are several over-the-counter products for this use, or in a pinch, you can use a bit of flour or cornstarch or place the nail into a softened bar of soap. Make sure that all bleeding has stopped before you leave your bunny alone. If the nail continues to bleed for some time, it may require a vet visit.

Grooming Show Rabbits

If you're planning on showing your rabbit, be aware that grooming takes on a whole new dimension. Just wielding a brush and comb won't cut it if you want to compete with other show rabbits. Showing rabbits, especially at large rabbit shows, is very competitive, and breeders and exhibitors take their exhibition very, very seriously. The longer your rabbit's hair is, the more seriously you must take your grooming.

If you have long-wooled rabbits especially, the time you will have to budget on a daily basis for grooming will escalate rapidly. Don't think you can neglect your bunny for weeks and then make up for it the week of the show. A savvy judge will easily recognize the difference between the coat of a well-maintained rabbit owned by a serious competitor and the coat of one that lives with a casual exhibitor.

The supplies necessary for grooming a show rabbit are much the same as for a pet, with the exception of a hair dryer. Instead, you will need to purchase a high-velocity pet dryer designed to blow room temperature air at a very high rate of speed. Unlike human hair dryers that blow hot air, a pet air dryer will separate each individual fiber of coat and will blow out dander and dust from the coat, without pulling out fur or overheating the skin. If you don't want to invest in a professional dryer, you can use a shop vacuum or canister vacuum cleaner set on reverse. It's much noisier than a regular dryer, so you might want to invest in a longer hose so you can put the vacuum cleaner behind a door or at least farther away from your bunny while you're grooming.

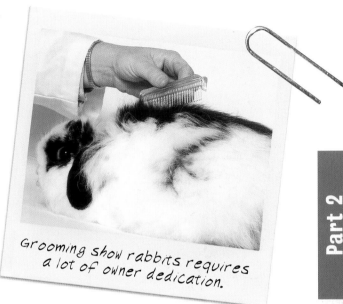

Grooming show rabbits requires a lot of owner dedication.

Dedication is a key word when showing rabbits. You must be dedicated to good grooming practices as well as feeding and taming. You should eliminate mats before they have a chance to begin. Be aware that you cannot create a show coat on a pet-bred rabbit. Good coats are bred, not made. Unless you start with a good-quality coat that you treat with care and respect, you will never be competitive at rabbit shows.

Grooming the Molting Rabbit

Some breeds of rabbits go through regular molting cycles. The Angora, for instance, molts about every two to three months. You will know he is going into a molt when you start finding more tangles when you comb him, and there will be more hair in the comb after your grooming sessions. You'll notice an increase in the amount of "fuzz" around his cage too, as his wool comes out by the handfuls. At this point, you will have to either hand-pluck your rabbit completely or shear him with clippers.

Some breeds, such as this English Angora, go through molting cycles.

Another Benefit of Grooming

Remember—grooming isn't just for beauty's sake. Grooming also serves as a bonding time between you and your rabbit, as well as a time that you can monitor his health and physical well-being.

Hand-Plucking Your Rabbit

Plucking his wool is just what it sounds like—it involves taking your thumb and forefinger and gently plucking out the dead wool. However, there should be no reason for a rabbit with a normal or plush coat to ever be sheared or plucked. If you decide to hand-pluck, you should plan on spending a lot more time than usual with your bunny each day. Starting in the middle of his back, you should hold the skin flat with one hand and, using your thumb and first finger of the other hand, gently pull away a section of wool, pulling from the tip.

Plucking the dead hair is not painful, if done correctly. By the time you've plucked a spot the size of a quarter, you'll be able to see the new wool undercoat already coming back in. From that point, it will be easier to pluck, as you can see the difference in the old and the new coats. All of the rabbit's body, including his belly, cheek, and chin (on the varieties that grow wool there) will have to be plucked.

If you don't like the idea of plucking the wool, you can use clippers to shear it, much like a sheep is sheared. Never put clippers directly against your rabbit's body. Always place a comb against the skin and cut the wool on the topside of the comb. A rabbit's skin is like tissue paper, and you can cut horrible gashes in it before you realize it.

You can also do a combination of plucking and shearing. Pluck the "good" wool and shear away the matted dirty wool. You'll have to experiment to see whether your rabbit prefers to have the hair on his face and sensitive areas plucked or sheared. Just do whatever he feels is the most comfortable. The end result for either will look the same as soon as the new hair gets a little length. If you're lucky, you'll have access to someone who can spin and weave it for you when you've saved enough.

Diet and Nutrition

Like humans, rabbits need a balanced, varied diet in order to obtain the necessary nutrients to stay healthy. Their diet requires more than just processed pellets. In order to provide a diet that will promote the optimum health of your rabbit, you need to give him vegetables, fruit, and most importantly, roughage every day in addition to a pellet diet.

Pellets

Pelleted food should always be fresh (if you buy in large quantities, you should put a large part of the food in your freezer for storage) and high in fiber (18 percent minimum fiber) but low in protein, as rabbits do not need processed fat. Remember, they are vegetarians in the wild.

Rabbits need a balanced, varied diet to stay healthy.

Pellets are acceptable as a base diet but need to be supplemented with other healthy foods.

Many well-meaning rabbit owners allow the appearance of a rabbit food to make their decision for them when shopping for their bunny. When choosing between boring gray pellets and a bright package that is filled with colorful bits and pieces, the eye obviously gravitates away from the gray pellets. You should learn to read labels; these may surprise you with findings of nuts, corn, grain products, and sometimes even animal by-products, none of which are good for your rabbit.

Although your rabbit will likely eat this food happily, leaving his dull-looking brown or green pellets behind, you should liken this behavior to a child choosing a sugar-sweetened, candy-coated cereal over oatmeal or other healthier breakfast cereals. Do the right thing and choose a rabbit pellet for your rabbit's daily diet that meets the specifications your veterinarian suggests for your particular rabbit's needs.

Any adequate rabbit pellet will have at least 18 percent fiber content, less than 14-15 percent protein, very low (maximum 1 percent) calcium levels, and should be hay or grass-based with absolutely no animal by-products. Depending on the weight and size of the adult rabbit, you should regulate the amount of food he receives daily instead of free feeding all he can hold. As a rule of thumb, give about 1/4 cup per 5-7 lb rabbit, 1/2 cup for 8-10 lb rabbits, and 3/4 cup for 11-15 lb rabbits. Older rabbits should be fed a pellet based on timothy hay, while younger rabbits seem to do fine on alfalfa-based pellets.

You will find that there is not nearly the selection of foods on the market for our rabbit friends as you will find for your cats, dogs, birds, or other house pets. Be sure you supplement any rabbit's diet of pellets with the correct amount of vegetables and fruits and the occasional addition of a few well-chosen treats. If you prefer to not feed pellets at all, your rabbit can be maintained on a natural diet of vegetables and fruits, so long as he is given unlimited quantities of good-quality hay.

Roughage and the Importance of Fiber

The most important element of a rabbit's diet is roughage. Fiber is a necessity for a rabbit's digestive system to function properly; in fact, rabbits are designed to eat and digest a vegetarian diet high in fiber. Their digestive system is much like that of a horse, allowing them to achieve a maximum nutrition via a diet that consists of high fiber and little, if any, protein.

Unfortunately, many foods that are high in fiber have very little nutritional value. For many generations, rabbits have been fed a diet that consists strictly of processed pellets, with the occasional vegetable or fruit treat. While pellets do have fiber, it is (in most foods) finely ground and, therefore, does far less for a rabbit's digestive system than the roughage and fiber found in grass hays. Because roughage also will help with the prevention of hairballs and obstructions in the digestive system that most rabbits seem prone to developing, the case is strong for feeding a diet higher in fiber and roughage than a rabbit can get from a diet consisting solely of pellets. Pellets can certainly be included in a rabbit's diet, but fresh grass hay and the correct vegetables should be the main part of a rabbit's diet–not just an occasional treat.

To keep your bunny's digestive system working properly, hay should be offered in large quantities on a constant basis and should be given far more credit than for just being chewing entertainment. It is very important that your rabbit get as much access to hay as possible. In the wild, rabbits exist on a diet that consists mainly of grass, which is, in its dry form, hay. In addition to the invaluable fiber it contains, hay also provides

Rabbits don't need pellets if their diet is filled with fruits, vegetables, and unlimited amounts of hay.

Hay should be offered to your rabbit in large quantities on a constant basis.

Apple Tree Twigs

Apple tree twigs provide good roughage, and most rabbits will consider them a special treat. (Don't tell him it's good for him!)

vitamins, minerals, and protein in a form the rabbit's digestive tract needs for its continued good health.

Grass hay or timothy hay are the better choices (fed in long strings instead of the chopped bales usually sold in pet stores), although some alfalfa hay is acceptable. Because alfalfa is found in most commercial rabbit pellets, it's not a good idea to feed only alfalfa hay, as it is higher in protein and calcium, which can overload your rabbit's system.

Most farm-supply stores can direct you to someone who sells bales of hay. Some pet stores sell bagged hay–even though this is not fresh, it is preferable to the small bales of shredded hay. Straw should not be fed, as it has no nutritional value.

Fruits and Vegetables

In addition to roughage, you should also feed your rabbit at least three kinds of vegetables daily, as well as a sampling of fruits. (Avoid sugary fruits except as rare treats.)

Vegetables

When shopping for vegetables for your bunny, you should choose a variety. Look for both dark, leafy vegetables and root vegetables (and the tops of some root veggies such as carrots). Stay away from beans and rhubarb. Make sure one vegetable each day contains vitamin A (indicated in the following list by an asterisk*). Add one vegetable to the diet at a time so you will know what foods your rabbit cannot tolerate. Eliminate the vegetable if it causes soft stools or diarrhea.

The following are vegetables that are safe and healthy for your rabbit.

Carrots and carrot tops are healthy vegetables for rabbits.

• Alfalfa, radish, and clover sprouts

• Basil

- Beet greens (tops)*

- Bok choy

- Broccoli (mostly leaves/stems)*

- Brussels sprouts

- Carrot and carrot tops*

- Celery

- Cilantro

- Clover

- Collard greens*

- Dandelion greens and flowers*

- Endive*

- Escarole

- Green peppers

- Kale *

- Mint

- Mustard greens*

- Parsley*

- Green pea pods (the flat, edible kind)*

- Peppermint leaves

- Radicchio

- Radish tops

- Raspberry leaves

- Romaine lettuce (no iceberg or light-colored leaf lettuce)*

- Spinach (feed rarely and sparingly)*

- Watercress*

- Wheat grass

Part 2

Fruits

You should feed your rabbit a sampling of fruits along with roughage and vegetables. Sugary fruits, such as bananas and grapes, should be fed sparingly and only as occasional treats. Bunnies have a sweet tooth, and just like most human children, will choose sugary foods over healthful ones if left to make their own choices.

Part 2

Remove the stem and seeds from apples before feeding.

Poison Control

If you suspect your rabbit has ingested an unsafe plant, please call your vet and your local poison control center or the ASPCA Animal Poison Control Center at

1-888-426-4435.

The following are fruits recommended for rabbits.

- Apple (remove stem and seeds)

- Blueberries

- Melon

- Orange (include the peel)

- Papaya

- Peach

- Pear

- Pineapple

- Plums

- Raspberries

- Strawberries

Age Considerations for Diet

A rabbit's diet also varies according to his age. Adult rabbits have different needs than babies, and these needs should be taken into account when deciding what to feed your rabbit.

Baby Rabbits

Baby rabbits can have unlimited access to pellets (available at all times), decreasing to 1/2 cup per 6 lbs of body weight by around 6 months.

From four to seven weeks of age, a baby rabbit should have access to his mother's milk and also be introduced to alfalfa hay and pellets. From seven weeks to seven months, unlimited pellets and unlimited hay can be provided. Do not feed fruits or vegetables to very young rabbits, except possibly as special (rare) treats. After 12 weeks of age, you can begin to introduce a few fruits and vegetables into your bunny's diet. Start out slowly, feeding no more than 1/2 oz of anything new until you can see how well your rabbit can tolerate the food changes. Gradually increase the amounts, but be sure you feed only one vegetable or fruit at a time. Don't add anything different for a few days, so you will know for certain what the culprit is if something upsets his stomach.

From four to seven weeks of age, a rabbit should consume his mother's milk and alfalfa hay.

Seven Months to One Year of Age

From seven months to a year of age, you should introduce timothy hay and grass hay and decrease alfalfa hay. You should also decrease the amount of pellets they are given on a daily basis, too, and increase the amounts of daily vegetables. Fruits should still be given on a rationed basis, no more than 1 to 2 oz per 6 lbs of body weight.

One Year to Five Years of Age

From the age of one year to about five years, your rabbit should get unlimited amounts of timothy grass and oat hay. Pellets should be fed on a ratio of 1/4 to 1/2 cup of

From one to five years of age, feed 1/4 to 1/2 cup of pellets per 6 lbs of body weight.

pellets and a minimum of 2 cups of chopped vegetables per 6 lbs of body weight. Fruit should still be given on a non-regular basis, no more than 2 oz per day.

Middle-Aged and Elderly Rabbits

The middle-aged bunny (more than six years of age) should continue the adult diet if sufficient weight is maintained. The amount of pellets can be varied to keep weight at a good average. Geriatric rabbits or rabbits with health problems may need unrestricted pellets to help keep their weight up. Alfalfa can be given to underweight rabbits, but only if calcium levels are normal. Annual blood workups are highly recommended for geriatric rabbits before they deviate from their regular diet.

Litter Box Training

Rabbits are very clean animals by nature, and in the wild, they will frequently use one spot far from their sleeping area to answer nature's call. Similarly, rabbits will often eliminate in the same spot in their cages, and most can be taught to use a litter box. However, one common mistake among rabbit owners is thinking that a rabbit is going to be like a cat and know instinctively where he is supposed to eliminate.

Be forewarned that if you are expecting such dedication from your new pet, perhaps you really should consider getting a cat instead. Most rabbits do not automatically realize what the box in the corner filled with pellets or other litter should be used for and will have to be trained to use a litter

Rabbits frequently use the same spot in their cages to eliminate.

If you use straw or hay as litter, you will need a litter box with higher sides.

box. And don't be surprised if, until he figures it out, he uses the litter box for sleeping or storing toys instead of what it was intended for. In fact, it is actually a good sign if you see him spending a lot of time in his litter pan, because if he is happy there, he will eventually begin to use it for its original purpose.

Purchasing a Litter Box

You don't have to purchase an expensive litter box; most people find that plastic shoeboxes work well for small rabbits, using larger sizes for larger rabbits. For giant breeds you can use a dog litter pan or even the bottom part of a travel cage. Some people report having excellent luck using a covered cat litter box. However, others say that these work better as a den or nest box for their bunny, and they prefer using an uncovered box as a litter pan. If you use hay or straw in the litter box, you will need to have a box with higher sides to keep the materials inside. Some plastic dog beds have high sides, with one shorter side for easier access for the bunny. Take a walk through a department store or pet supermarket and use your imagination.

Choosing the Right Litter

Choosing the pan that's going to be acceptable to your bunny is only half the battle. You still must find a suitable litter that he will find interesting but not appetizing (unless you are using hay in his litter tray, which is completely safe). Experiment with different litters in different pans and see which one your rabbit prefers.

There are many suitable choices for use in your rabbit's litter pan. Cat litters made from recycled newspaper and wood are excellent and absorbent choices. The House Rabbit Society recommends organic and thus safely edible litters, made from alfalfa, oat, citrus, or paper. Be wary, however, if you find your rabbit eating a lot of any alfalfa or oat litter, as they can expand and cause bloating.

Almost any dust-free, unscented cat litter can, in fact, be used safely, including the usual clay litters, as long as they do not claim to be "clumping." Because many bunnies like to

Choosing Safe Litter Material

Choose a litter that will be safe for your bunny, because he will probably spend a lot of time sitting in his litter tray. This includes:

- Litters made from aspen bark
- Wooden pellets for use in woodstoves
- Litter made from recycled newspapers
- Newspaper with hay sprinkled over the top
- Dust-free clay cat litter
- Unscented cat litter

Don't choose a litter that may clump and cause a blockage if it is inhaled or ingested. Corncob bedding should not be used as a litter, as it may appear appetizing to your bunny but is indigestible and likely to create intestinal blockages that will require surgery to fix. Cedar and pine shavings or sawdust are not very absorbent, don't control odors well, and the oils in these have been known to create liver damage or respiratory problems. Read the labels—if the litter contains zinc oxide, it should not be used as litter for your rabbit. Don't choose a scented litter, as some of the deodorant crystals are very toxic to rabbits.

dig and play in their litter, the "clumping" litters can not only cause respiratory problems, but they can also create a fatal blockage in your rabbit's air passageways if the litter "clumps" inside them, or it can also cause an intestinal blockage if your rabbit ingests the clumps. Using a dust-free and unscented clay litter is important, as rabbits are prone to respiratory problems that can be exacerbated by the dust and scents in some cat litters, and many of the deodorant crystals in scented litters are very toxic to rabbits.

Many rabbit owners stock up on woodstove pellets each fall and winter and use these in their rabbit litter trays throughout the year. They are economical and safe. Some people find that just putting a layer of newspaper in the litter tray and covering it with hay works well for their rabbits, although this has no odor-controlling qualities.

No matter what litter you choose, you may wish to sprinkle some of your rabbit's food pellets in with the litter (don't worry, he won't eat the soiled ones) to make it more interesting for him to be in his box and entice him to mark it as "home."

Creative Litter Boxes

If your rabbit doesn't like the traditional tray you have chosen for his litter pan, be creative. The following are some other containers you can use as your rabbit's litter pan.

• A basket lined with a heavy-duty garbage bag (he will chew the basket, so it will serve double duty as a toy and a litter pan)

• A heavy-duty cardboard box lined with a garbage bag

• A covered cat-litter box

• The bottom half of your rabbit's travel cage

• A shallow-glass baking dish (works great for dwarf bunnies)

• A wooden box, custom designed for his cage

You should also change your rabbit's litter tray on a regular basis, usually every day or so. Rinse the tray well with warm, soapy water and follow this with a white vinegar rinse to eliminate odors that may have soaked into the tray. If you have a lot of calcium buildup from urine, you should soak the tray in undiluted white vinegar.

Litter Box Placement

If your bunny will have free range of the house without spending time in a cage, it will be a little harder to figure out where to place the litter box. You may simply have to be prepared to clean up an accident or two as you wait until he decides on his designated "bathroom area."

First, place one litter tray near his bed and another in a corner. Most rabbits like privacy, and they will naturally go to a corner or other hidden area, such as behind a piece of furniture or behind long draperies. To entice the bunny to the right location, place a few of his droppings and a urine-soaked paper towel there. (As you clean up accidents, you can put the paper towels in a zippered plastic bag for use as a training tool later.) If he doesn't take the hint, you may have to move the litter tray to the place your rabbit has chosen. Even if this means temporarily rearranging furniture, it may be easier than trying to change your rabbit's mind. You can try moving it a tiny bit each day until you eventually get it moved to where you wanted it to begin with. However, don't be surprised if one day your bunny realizes that he's been duped and he begins to again mark the location he first wanted.

If you are using a cage, it's a good idea to put more than one litter box in the cage to begin with. This way, you stand a better chance of having your rabbit immediately beginning to use at least one of them. Once you can see which box he prefers, simply remove the others for use in his exercise area as soon as he is ready to be trusted in a larger space.

The First Few Days of Training

The first few days of litter training are crucial. You should be willing to spend as much time as possible supervising your pet, offering encouragement and praise when he uses his box correctly, and providing gentle corrections when he does not. You can't plan on doing a lot of other things while you're housetraining a bunny. It takes constant supervision. Remember that good toilet habits are easier to form correctly than they are to change or correct later. The time you spend on it now is well worth it.

It is easier to train an adult rabbit than it is to train a baby, especially an adult that is neutered or spayed and is relaxed and comfortable in his environment. Toilet training a rabbit that is not neutered or spayed is very difficult, as these rabbits can become quite hormonal on a regular basis and feel the need to mark everything in their reach, claiming their territory with both urine and droppings.

See Where Your Rabbit Goes On His Own

There is no need to put a litter box in a cage and expect your rabbit to use it immediately. Instead, just watch to see where he eliminates by his own

Offer your rabbit lots of praise when he uses his litter box correctly.

Slow Learner?

Although it's frustrating when your bunny refuses to listen to reason and continues to eliminate wherever he wants, it is important that you continue to be patient. As with humans, some rabbits are just slower learners and may take longer to get the message. There are also other factors that can be contributing to your rabbit's lack of cooperation.

Some rabbits are simply more territorial, so they may feel a need to mark a wider space. Another possibility may be that you've given your rabbit too much area and not enough litter boxes, or perhaps you haven't had your bunny spayed or neutered, and he or she is feeling particularly hormonal right now. (A bunny that is fighting raging hormones is a toilet-training nightmare!)

The problem could also be with the litter box itself. Maybe the sides are too high on the litter box and your bunny finds it uncomfortable to get in and out. Perhaps the sides are too low and he doesn't feel that he's getting enough privacy. Be patient, try to think like a bunny, and you may find that he's smarter than you gave him credit for.

choice the first time and then place the box there. The chances are extremely good that he will continue to use this same spot forever, at least to urinate. Most will use it for depositing their feces as well, although sometimes, if they are frightened or upset, they will eliminate without meaning to. Just put a layer of newspaper under the cage to catch any stray droppings.

When you see your bunny crouch, pushing out his bottom and tail, it is a signal that he is about to urinate. If he is in the right place (his litter tray), wait until he is finished; then praise him and give him a treat. If he isn't in the tray, say, "No" firmly, and coax him to his tray with his favorite treat. However, make sure you never yell at your rabbit. Not only is this harsh, but it can also startle him enough to make him lose his bladder, enforcing a behavior exactly the opposite of what you intended.

Wait to see where your rabbit eliminates, and put his litter box there.

He will likely sit in the tray and eat the treat and then finish eliminating there. Once you've managed to get him to go to the bathroom in the correct place and his odors are in that place, he will be more likely to continue to claim that area by marking it with both feces and urine.

Safe Haven

You want your rabbit to think of his cage as a safe haven away from the rest of the world. To ensure that he continues to think this way and therefore will try to keep his cage clean (using his litter tray for a bathroom), you should follow these guidelines.

• Respect your bunny's privacy—don't pull him out of his den or cage against his will

• Don't put your bunny into his cage as a punishment. Make sure he always goes in of his own choice.

• Don't clean the cage while the bunny is inside it.

• Don't do things to him that he doesn't like while he's in his cage.

Remember, dogs, cats, and other animals require weeks of constant supervision to become fairly consistently litter trained, too. Don't give up if your rabbit seems to be ignoring your best efforts.

Make It Pleasant

Your rabbit is more likely to use his litter pan if you make it pleasant for him by putting hay, his food bowl, toys, or treats inside it. Because rabbit litter pans aren't as smelly as those of other animals, don't panic if you see

Litter Box Training Tips

• If your rabbit enjoys kicking the litter out of his box, try using a different type of litter. If it still happens, get a box with higher sides. You can also try using a covered litter box for cats.

• Some rabbits seem to be attracted to the human's bathroom for their own potty times. If you have a fluffy rug near the toilet, you may find that your rabbit is using it as his toilet. If you remove the rug (disinfect it thoroughly to remove the odors before you put it back in place) and place a small litter box in the near area with a paper towel soaked in your rabbit's urine inside of it, your rabbit will likely begin using it.

• Sometimes rabbits will choose a spot on a rug even if it isn't in your bathroom. In that case, you may have to remove the rug until your rabbit takes up a different habit. If it's a small rug and you're not particular about where it is, you might put the rug wherever you want the rabbit to "go," and put the litter pan on top of it.

• Because rabbits use their toilet habits as a way to mark their territory, you may find that they will want to mark your favorite chair, couch, or bed. This is their way of claiming you and your favorite things as theirs. If you find your rabbit is inhibiting your access to these pieces of furniture, you will have to train them to stay off them entirely. Most rabbits can learn "no" or "off" if you consistently use it. Firmly make your rabbit get off your furniture as you say it. If he doesn't learn to stay off, you may have to just block off the rooms that contain furniture your bunny is abusing. You can also cover the furniture with a piece of plastic or newspaper, that your bunny will find uncomfortable.

• Keep your bunny in a small territory until he has proven himself to you. Don't worry so much about pellet accidents, but be firm about controlling urine accidents.

• Have your bunny spayed or neutered as soon as possible to eliminate problems with territorial spraying. It's hard enough to litter train a bunny without adding the problem of hormonal surges to the equation.

your bunny sitting, sleeping, or eating in it. It's normal for them to spend time there, even when they're not using it as it was intended. Never disturb your bunny when he's in his litter pan, no matter what he's doing there.

Once your rabbit is using his litter pan reliably in his cage, you can gradually give him more and more free time in the house. Just be sure that whatever room he's in has a litter box (or two). When you're not at home to supervise him, put your bunny in his cage, or in a small, uncarpeted area that will make accident cleanup simpler.

Part 2

Let your rabbit go back to his cage on his own when training.

Your Rabbit's Home Is His Castle

Don't think that because you find rabbit wastes all over his cage that your rabbit is refusing to become litter box trained. Instead, he is simply identifying the cage as his home, his property. Just as a small child grabs a toy and announces, "Mine!" so does a rabbit mark his territory. We humans sometimes don't understand this, though, because rabbits don't use words; they use actions. This marking of territory is actually a very good thing, as it means that when he goes out into the big world (ie: other parts of your home) he will distinguish between what is "yours" and what is "his" and not try to mark your territory as his own.

To further reinforce this action, it is very important that you allow your rabbit's cage to be his castle–don't do anything to him inside his cage that he does not like. You must respect the cage as truly his, so that he will feel safe and secure there and continue to mark it as his territory, instead of marking his territory outside of it. Don't force him to leave it; instead, coax him out of it with treats that he loves. Don't clean his cage while he is in it, as he will see this action as you trying to take over ownership of his property, and he will reciprocate by looking elsewhere for "his space" (likely someplace that has a lot of your scent, such as your favorite chair or bed).

Don't pick him up and put him back in his cage when his exercise time is over. If he is enjoying being loose in his exercise yard, he will see this action as his cage not being a home but a prison. Instead, place a treat he really likes inside his cage and let him go back into his cage of his own will, or gently herd him back into his cage, so that in your rabbit's mind he's "escaping" into the safety of his cage. Never chase him or trap him and put him back in his cage.

This same theory applies if your rabbit doesn't live in a cage but calls a particular part of a room "home." Don't trespass into that area. Let it truly be "his" and you will find that most rabbits will housetrain themselves to keep their home clean.

Accidents Happen

Accidents will happen, and your rabbit may eliminate somewhere other than in his litter box, but you should *never* punish your rabbit for having an accident. It isn't really his fault; he's just being a normal bunny. Very few bunnies use their urine or feces as a punishment for their humans, so if a rabbit has an accident away from his litter box, the problem can in fact usually be traced back to something that you did incorrectly. Perhaps you didn't notice where he really wanted to go, and you placed his tray in the wrong place, or perhaps you upset him while he was away from his box and a few pellets "leaked out" without his being able to stop it. Maybe a child, dog, or loud noise frightened him. In any case, accidents are perfectly normal, and most rabbits don't have total control over their feces anyway.

It is completely normal for accidents to happen outside of your rabbit's cage.

If your bunny has an accident, especially a urine accident, on your carpet or upholstered furniture, it is very important to clean it up quickly and eliminate the odor immediately, effectively, and permanently so he will not come to believe this is an acceptable place for him to relieve himself.

Wipe the area with a cloth soaked in sodium bicarbonate or diluted white vinegar. Both of these will neutralize the smell of urine. If the accident occurred on linoleum or other solid flooring, mop with warm, soapy water followed by a rinse of undiluted white vinegar to eliminate the stain as well as odor. Rabbit urine is very strong, so it can easily (and permanently) stain painted surfaces, fabrics, etc. Therefore, it is important to clean it up quickly and effectively.

If your bunny drops waste pellets, just pick them up with a tissue and flush them down the toilet (or place in his litter tray to show him where he *should* have eliminated instead). You can also vacuum up any wastes that are in the wrong place, but be sure to empty your vacuum cleaner bag or canister before the pellets have time to mold and become smelly.

Part 2

Change the Litter Box Often

You should change the litter in your rabbit's tray every one or two days and rinse the tray well with warm, soapy water. If you start seeing a lot of calcium buildup on the bottom from urine, you can remove this by soaking it in undiluted white vinegar.

If your rabbit puts wastes in his food dish, he is just marking his territory.

When Accidents Signal a Problem

If you notice that your bunny is dribbling urine frequently, it is time for a vet checkup. Some bunnies are prone to urinary tract infections or bladder problems. This is a warning sign of that, so be certain you get your rabbit to a veterinarian as soon as possible.

Sometimes rabbits will start eliminating just outside their litter trays, which can be very frustrating for you. This could either be a signal that your rabbit is distressed about something (perhaps a new bunny or other pet in the area, or you've cleaned his tray with a cleanser that irritates his sensitive nose–this is why you should never use anything other than mild soap and vinegar when cleaning their tray). For whatever reason, you can see this action as your bunny "underlining" his ownership of the cage. You can either place another litter box against the original one until he chooses one or the other to use, or put newspapers in that area to absorb the accidents until he stops the annoying habit.

Mistaken Identity

You may notice that there are food pellets in your rabbit's litter pan and waste pellets in his food dish. Don't worry–your rabbit isn't going through some sort of identity crisis, and he hasn't lost his mind. This is normal behavior. In fact, because they notice that their rabbit is placing food pellets in his litter tray, many people simply use only food pellets instead of regular litter in the litter pan. It's certainly an economical choice! At farm feed-type stores, you may find that rabbit food in a 50 lb bag is cheaper than any other litter choices! Putting wastes in his food dish is just your rabbit's way of warning everyone, "This food dish is mine; stay away."

The Importance of Consistency

The key word to litter training is consistency. Leave the litter boxes in place once your rabbit is using them effectively. Don't wash them with different cleansers, and continue to praise him when he uses a box correctly and correct him gently when he does not. Keep your eyes open for signs of an illness or disease that might cause housetraining "backsliding." Remember, once a rabbit is housetrained, it doesn't mean that the job is done forever. Many rabbits do forget their training from time to time. Just use the same methods you used successfully the first time, and you'll get him back on track in no time.

Litter Box

If you must move your rabbit's cage for some reason, allow him to decide where inside the cage he wants to go to the bathroom now that the cage is in a new location, and move the box there. It may be that he originally chose the previous side because it provided a more secure feeling, and now that the cage has been moved, that side is nearer the door. Perhaps the box was nearer a window where he enjoyed looking outdoors while he rested. Whatever the reason, your rabbit will ultimately have to make the decision about litter box placement before he will agree to use it consistently.

Part 2

Interpreting Bunny Behavior

There's an old joke with a punch line that basically says, "Before you can train the dog, you have to know more than the dog." There's more truth to that statement than humor. Before we can train our pets, we have to know more about them than they realize about themselves. In other words, we have to understand their behaviors, be one step ahead of them, be ready to offer firm but gentle corrections, and offer positive reinforcement to aim their behavior in a direction we can live with. The same idea applies to training your rabbit. Before you can train your rabbit, you have to be able to understand why he behaves the way he does.

Before people can train rabbits, they have to be able to understand rabbit behaviors.

Many rabbit behaviors that are perceived as "bad" are really normal and natural.

Rabbits Will Be Rabbits

It is important for any pet owner to realize that many times what is perceived as a bad behavior on the part of an animal may, in fact, be simply the animal doing what comes naturally to him. Rabbits will be rabbits. For instance, keep in mind that they chew incessantly (especially during adolescence), they don't have total bowel control so may continue to leave droppings in your home even when they're thoroughly litter box trained, and they will never be brave and outgoing.

Remember that in a rabbit's natural world, everything larger than him (and even some smaller) is a predator, while he is a threat to no one himself. Therefore, rabbits learned eons ago that if "fight" was not their forte, it must be "flight." This behavior is ingrained in a rabbit, and there is nothing we can do to change it. All we can do is make our rabbits feel as comfortable and secure as possible and provide him with enough proper chew toys to soothe his cravings.

Interpreting Bunny Body Language

While it's true that English is our primary language, it's important that you now become fluent in "Rabbit." You won't have to worry about pronouns and verb usage, but it can be just as difficult to interpret (and admittedly impossible to write). Each hop, kick, and grunt that a rabbit makes is trying to tell you something. Just keep your eyes and ears open and learn.

Sniffing

Sniffing may mean that he's annoyed with you, or he could be just talking to you.

Grunts

Grunts are usually the signal of a very angry bunny.

Sniffing is your rabbit's way of talking to you.

Shrill Scream

This means that your bunny is in trouble. Get help. Expect to find a bunny that's in pain.

Bumping Into You or Licking You

These are definite signs of affection and trust.

Circling Your Feet

Usually done by an unneutered bunny, this is usually seen as a sexual behavior.

Spraying

Males that are not neutered will mark female rabbits in this manner, as well as their territory. Females will also spray.

Chinning

(Rubbing their chins on different humans and items.) A rabbit's chin contains scent glands, so they rub their chin on items to indicate that they belong to them.

Bunny Hop/Dance

This is a sign of pure happiness. Only the very happiest of bunnies will let you see this expression of abject joy.

Lunging At a Person or Other Bunny

This is a warning to "back off!" Your rabbit could be feeling fearful or angry.

Territory Droppings

Droppings that are not in a pile but are scattered are signs that this territory belongs to the rabbit. This will often occur upon entering a new environment.

Playing

Rabbits like to push or toss objects around. They may also race madly around the house, jump on and off of the couch, and act like a kid who has had too much sugar.

A bunny hop or dance is a sign of true happiness.

Stomping usually means that your rabbit is frightened or mad.

Rearranging His Cage After You've Cleaned

Your rabbit is saying, "Don't touch my stuff." Rabbits are creatures of habit, and when they get things just right, they like them to remain that way.

Stomping

He's frightened, mad, or trying to tell you that there's danger (in his opinion). He may also have an empty food dish or water bottle.

Squeaks

Higher-pitched than grunts and usually more rapid, these squeaks are often accompanied by cowering in a corner or running around the cage and are definite signs of anxiety, nervousness, and/or fear.

Teeth Grinding

Mild grinding indicates contentment, like a cat's purr. Loud grinding can indicate pain.

The Ears Have It

The positioning of your rabbit's ears are great indicators as to what your rabbit is thinking or feeling.

Ears Straight Up (Lop Ears Go Forward)

Your bunny is thinking, "Look at that!" or "Did you hear that?" This often indicates surprise or mischievous plans.

Ears Flat

If his eyes are closed or he is stretched out, he's saying, "I'm resting." It can also mean "I'm angry" if he is grunting at you.

One Ear Forward, One Back

This indicates a rabbit that is semi-attentive but not completely interested yet, as if he's saying, "Hmmm...very interesting." When the ears go forward or straight up, then he is interested.

One ear forward and one back indicates that your rabbit is only somewhat interested.

If your bunny's ears go straight up, it shows that he is surprised or interested.

Behavior Problems and Solutions

When He Bites the Hand That Feeds Him

Although rabbits are usually docile creatures that adapt well to a loving family situation, occasionally you may come across a rabbit that has been mistreated in a previous home or has suffered other stressful situations that have made him very wary of humans. Many times, a rabbit has learned aggressive tendencies to cope with a problem in his home life. If small children persisted in picking him up, possibly dropping him, carrying him around, and not allowing him any time to just be a bunny, it is only natural for him to learn that the only way to be left alone is to inflict pain on his tormenter.

As soon as he discovered that if he bit or scratched he was released to do as he pleased, he began using this as a defense mechanism. If no one in his family cared enough to fix the problem immediately and teach all family members to read rabbit body language, the problem was just allowed to get worse as time went on. Although it is hard to raise the trust level of a suspicious rabbit, it's certainly not impossible. Just be armed with a steady supply of patience.

Solutions

The first thing to do with a vicious bunny is to take him to the vet to rule out any medical factors that might be causing his displays of aggressive behavior. Rabbits that are in pain will be extremely aggressive in order to avoid more pain. Your rabbit-savvy vet will know to check for mites, fleas, wounds, burrs, or internal parasites that may be causing your pet discomfort.

While you're at the vet, you can take care of the second order of business (if it hasn't already been done) and have your pet spayed or neutered. Many non-spayed females in particular will become ultra-territorial and will display very aggressive behavior defending their home or possessions.

Your rabbit should visit the vet if he displays frequent aggressive behaviors.

If your pet doesn't calm down after his surgery, it's time for behavior modification practices. Now is the time that it becomes necessary to know more than the rabbit! You will have to convince the angry bunny that aggressive behavior is not only nonproductive and unnecessary but unacceptable as well. This doesn't mean using force to bend the rabbit to your will (something that is impossible to do in the first place) but instead training the bunny to make the right decisions, with just a little coaxing from you. Behavior modification means teaching him that he will be happier if he does not display aggressive tendencies, because he will make his humans happier, and in turn those humans will do nice things for him.

It is very hard to not lose your temper with the rabbit that just put a hole in your finger when you were trying to pick him up to let him out of his cage for free time, or to give him a snack, but it's important to remember that this is not a genetically vicious animal. Most likely, your rabbit is a victim of bad circumstances, and it is up to you to restore

Problems and How to Solve Them

Problem: Rabbit sprays urine all over the house, mounts his owner's leg and other rabbits, pulls out fur, and builds nests.

Solution: This is all sexual/mating behavior. Spay or neuter your rabbit.

Problem: Rabbit scratches or bites when he is picked up.

Solution: Don't pick him up until he is comfortable with it; it does no one any good to do so until he is ready. Open his cage door and let him come out on his own, and sit on the floor on his level to play with him. He feels very small and insignificant. Let him know that his feelings are important to you.

Problem: Rabbit is leaving droppings in his food dish.

Solution: Don't worry about it. It's normal behavior. He's just saying, "This is my dish."

Problem: Rabbit lunges at owner and tries to bite while in his cage.

Solution: You may have to try several things before you hit on the solution that fits your rabbit's problem, as this can be a signal of several different problems. First, in case this is a case of territorial raging hormones, you should spay or neuter your rabbit.

Once that is done, if the problem continues, make sure you are not scaring your rabbit unintentionally. Rabbits don't have good vision directly in front of them, so always approach from the side. Don't "swoop down" on top of your rabbit. When your rabbit lunges at you or tries to bite you, place your hand firmly on top of his head and rub between his eyes.

Problem: Rabbit continually moves things around in his cage.

Solution: Let him! It's his cage and his home. You arrange your house the way you want it; let him arrange his home the way he likes it and leave it the way he puts it. When you clean, be sure to put things back in their "proper" place.

Problem: Rabbit runs from you when he is approached.

Solution: Don't make any "predatory" moves toward your rabbit. Sit on the floor with your rabbit and let him make the overtures to you. Don't attempt to pick him up, because he may be learning that running from you and biting keeps him from being placed back in his cage. Put treats in his cage, and gently "herd" him back into the cage of his own volition.

Problem: A previously housetrained rabbit starts urinating outside his litter box.

Solution: If the rabbit is spayed/neutered and this doesn't seem to be a territorial display, a urinary or bladder problem may be the cause. See your veterinarian.

Problem: Rabbit is chewing furniture, wires, baseboards, and digging in carpet.

Solution: Provide him with proper chew toys and firmly correct him when he chews something that is not allowed. Tape up wires so they are out of your rabbit's reach. Rabbits are going to dig no matter where they are. If he is creating a problem by digging in your carpet, simply keep him out of carpeted areas.

Problem: A previously active bunny becomes withdrawn and quiet. A previously happy-go-lucky bunny displays aggressive behavior.

Solution: This warrants a trip to the vet, as any change in behavior can signal a health concern.

Problem: Rabbit spends a lot of time sitting in his litter box.

Solution: This isn't a problem. This is normal rabbit behavior and means he is a happy, well-adjusted rabbit that is going to be easily housetrained.

his faith in humans. One bout of lost temper on your part can undo weeks of dedication, so if you feel your temper slipping, just walk away and leave this rabbit alone (in a secure situation) until you are capable of working with him again and keeping a smile on your face. (It's true that animals can hear the smile in your voice, so always smile when you are talking to your pets, especially during training.)

Many times, just not reacting to their misbehavior can break the behavior pattern. Remember, this is a rabbit you're dealing with here, not an attack-trained Rottweiler. He may pinch you, he might even draw a drop of blood, but he will not be able to inflict lasting damage to you. If he bites you, instead of withdrawing your hand quickly (which is the desired effect), simply leave your hand there. Don't raise your voice, and continue talking to him as if nothing has happened. Imagine his confusion.

When he's done this in the past, his humans left him alone. However, this human isn't running. Doing this over a period of a few weeks will usually break a biting bunny's habit all by itself without any further training necessary. If possible, get other brave humans to practice this same treatment to let the bunny see that biting no longer has the power it once had over people.

It's best to spend a lot of extra time with shy rabbits.

Shy Behavior

If your bunny is timid, you will have to spend a lot of time with him, teaching him that humans are the "givers of good things" and that they will allow no harm to come to him. The easiest way to do this is to spend as much time as possible every day with the bunny on his terms. Don't force him to sit in your lap or do the things you want him to do, but provide him with a safe area where he can feel secure instead.

Solutions

For some people, a dog exercise pen (collapsible, usually allowing a 4' x 8' play area) is a great idea. Simply sit inside the pen with him (take along a pillow or two so you can get comfy) and do the things you normally do—read (a book, not a crackly newspaper or magazine) or talk on the telephone—while your rabbit does whatever he pleases.

Have some of his favorite toys inside, as well as snacks, bedding, a litter box, and a safe house (a small dog airline crate with no door works great) for him to escape to if he is frightened.

During this time, just sit with him. Don't attempt to pet him, and don't force him to do anything; just enjoy being with him and let him sense your pleasure. Soon his curiosity will get the better of him, and he will begin coming closer and closer. Eventually, he will be so comfortable with your presence that he will want to lie against you as he rests, and if you carry special treats in your pockets, he will learn to search them out.

Once the rabbit has come to you, it is time to reach out and touch him. If he flinches away, simply remove your hand and go back to what you were doing (reading, talking, etc.) Before long, he'll make another overture, and you can repeat the above until the time comes that he enjoys the caress.

Chewing

One of the most common problems owners have with their rabbits is their incessant chewing. Rabbits will often seek out furniture, shoes, and even more dangerous things, such as electrical wires–anything they can find. However, you should be aware that chewing isn't a behavior problem for a rabbit, but is instead just a natural part of being a rabbit. He doesn't have hands to pick things up and examine them as we humans do, so a rabbit's teeth become the way he explores the world around him through taste and texture. Chewing also promotes good health, as it keeps his teeth worn down (a rabbit's teeth grow continually throughout his lifetime) and helps him keep strong jaw muscles.

Chewing is a natural behavior for rabbits, not a behavior problem.

Chewing problems are much worse during adolescence, as the young rabbit explores the world around him. Although even a geriatric rabbit will still enjoy his chew toys, the desire to

Provide your rabbit with plenty of things he is allowed to chew.

sink his teeth into everything he comes into contact with will dissipate as he gets older. Keep reminding yourself of that when you find bunny-sized tooth marks on all of your furniture legs, shoes, belts, and books while your bunny is a teenager!

Solution

Unfortunately, there is no way to train your rabbit not to chew. Fish gotta swim, birds gotta fly, and rabbits gotta chew. The best you can do is provide your rabbit with good-quality chew toys to hopefully take care of his chewing needs, and rabbit-proof your home so that he cannot get to anything that isn't "bunny tooth proof." If you catch your rabbit chewing something he shouldn't, you should always make a firm (verbal) correction, and in rare cases, eventually a light bulb may go off. But don't count on it. It's far better to just move everything from his reach.

Digging

Many people request help for breaking a rabbit's habit of digging into their carpet. However, this is a rabbit's true nature again, just as chewing is. In the wild, a rabbit made his home beneath the surface of the earth. A house rabbit doesn't know the difference between "outdoors" and "inside"—all he knows is that nature tells him to burrow. So burrow he must.

Solution

Give your rabbit materials that are acceptable for him to burrow in—old T-shirts, blankets, and towels are great burrowing material. You can even create a playhouse with a carpet-covered floor and tunnel beneath it to give him the illusion that he created a burrow himself.

Raging Hormones

Rabbit behavior changes drastically as a rabbit matures. The baby rabbit that loved to be held and cuddled and would sit quietly in your lap for hours suddenly doesn't want you to even touch him, much less try to hold him.

Once a rabbit's hormones start to rage, that sweet little bunny can become a biting, urine-spraying, little hairy demon, destroying everything his teeth can fit around and totally forgetting everything he learned about housetraining. Either sex may circle your feet like a cat displaying mating behaviors but not want you to make any kind of response to their actions.

Solution

Spaying or neutering your bunny will help these behavior problems immensely. Also, when you're working with your rabbit on behavior modification practices, don't forget to reward good behavior. When your rabbit is playing quietly and behaving exactly as a good rabbit should, give him a treat to encourage more of

Spaying or neutering can help with hormonal behavior problems.

this behavior. Some rabbits respond well to small helpings of fruit or cereal, but limit the amount you give your rabbit because some rabbits can develop severe digestive upsets from these kinds of treats. Talk to your veterinarian about what kinds of treats your rabbit can safely enjoy.

Training and Activities for Your Rabbit

Though a rabbit cannot be trained to follow commands as obediently as dogs or cats, you can hand tame your rabbit very easily and give him the opportunity to safely go outdoors on a leash and harness. There are also many other fun activities you and your rabbit can participate in together, including traveling and showing your rabbit.

Training

The first training that any rabbit should receive from his owner is to be taught that he can trust you implicitly, no matter what. Be sure that you are always consistent in all your training, because any variations from routine can confuse your rabbit and will undo the advancements you've

Training and hand taming can be a fun activity for both you and your rabbit.

It is fairly easy to hand tame most rabbits.

made in his training. Never punish your rabbit or yell at him—only use positive training methods, offering him treats or praise as rewards when he performs correctly.

Hand Taming

Hand taming basically consists of letting your rabbit come to you on his own terms, teaching your rabbit that you won't harm him, and offering lots of positive reinforcement on a regular schedule.

It is your job to teach him that humans are friendly and that you will allow no harm to come to him. The easiest way to do this is to spend as much time as possible every day with the bunny on his terms. Don't force him to sit in your lap or do the things you want him to do, but provide him with a safe area where he can feel secure instead. For some people, a dog exercise pen (collapsible, usually allowing a 4' x 8' play area) is a great idea.

Simply sit inside the pen with him and do normal human things. Don't attempt to pet him, and don't force him to do anything. Soon his curiosity will get the better of him, and he will begin coming closer and closer. Eventually, he will be so comfortable with your presence that he will want to lie against you as he rests, and if you carry special treats in your pockets, he will learn to search them out.

Once the rabbit has come to you, it is time to reach out and touch him. If he flinches away, simply remove your hand and go back to what you were doing (reading, talking, etc.). Before long, he'll make another attempt, and you can repeat the above until the time comes that he enjoys the caress. Once he is comfortable with you petting him, reward him with treats or praise.

Leash and Harness Training

The purpose of putting a harness and leash on a rabbit is to give him an opportunity to safely visit the great outdoors, while being strictly supervised and kept secure. Walking a

Part 2

rabbit is not like walking a dog; most likely, he will not stay by your side obediently or stop when you tell him to. It is also not meant to serve as great exercise for either of you, but it does allow your rabbit to be outside and explore safely.

The first thing to remember when training a rabbit to wear a harness and walk on a leash is that you absolutely cannot walk a rabbit. The rabbit can, however, walk you. The best you can hope for is to train your rabbit to accept wearing a harness and accept having you on the end of his leash.

Leash training is a safe way for your rabbit to visit the outdoors.

Just put the harness on the rabbit, attach the leash, and follow him around. Remember—the rabbit will be walking you. Much of his time will be spent stopping to smell the roses, the grass, and plants. But you are giving your bunny a safe voyage into the great outdoors and at the same time allowing for some bonding time between you and your pet.

Traveling

Whether you're traveling across town to visit the vet or across the country to move to a new home, you should be aware that traveling is stressful for your bunny. Although every bunny handles stress differently and is stressed to different degrees by changes and upheavals in his life, you should do your best to make sure that your rabbit makes the move with as little trauma as possible.

You should let your rabbit get used to his travel cage well in advance of your travel date. Many people take the door off their plastic airline travel cage and let the bunny use it for a "den" inside his cage or exercise area. This is an excellent plan, as it feels like a "home away from home" for him if he has to spend any time traveling.

Automobile Travel

During mild temperatures, you won't have as much concern about traveling as you will have in the heat of summer or the cold of winter. Your rabbit may not eat much while he's

It's a good idea to let your rabbit get used to his travel cage in advance.

actually traveling, but you should put some hay and small pieces of apple or carrot in the carrier so he'll have something to nibble on if he should get hungry. A water bottle can be affixed to his travel cage so he won't have to worry about getting thirsty.

During summer or winter months, you should climate control your car before you load your bunny. Be careful not to let any air, warm or cold, blow directly on him, as this can cause respiratory ailments. If your rabbit is in a plastic airline-type travel cage, he will be better protected against drafts. If he travels in a wire cage, be sure to bring along a towel or blanket to cover his cage to avoid having him in a draft. If you are traveling in inclement weather or weather that is excessively hot or cold, you should take the proper precautions against having car trouble and carry along a cooler with the correct emergency items in it—frozen bottles of water for summer, bottles of hot water for winter, as well as a few extra treats. If you should have car trouble, you can put these warm or cold bottles in your rabbit's cage and keep him comfortable until help arrives.

Vacation? Things to Consider

You've spent the last few weeks or months planning your vacation, your reservations are made, your clothes are packed, and suddenly it hits you that there is one family member who hasn't been considered: your rabbit buddy. Another major decision suddenly looms, and questions await answers.

Could your vacation plans include your pet? Can your rabbit's psyche handle being boarded at a boarding facility? Do you have a neighbor or friend who would enjoy having a houseguest and would house/pet-sit while you're gone?

If you have a friend or neighbor who would be willing to either take your rabbit to his or her home for the duration of your vacation, stay in your home to rabbit-sit, or as a last-case scenario, come over daily to feed and water and allow your rabbit some free time, the problem is solved. If that isn't an option, you will either have to take your rabbit with you, find a safe, pleasant place for him to be boarded while you're gone, or cancel your plans.

Remember that your rabbit is "riding blind" in his cage. He can't see where you're going, he doesn't know the light is turning red, and he can't see the twists and turns ahead. Drive gently when he's in the car with you–no sudden stops and starts, and remember to take curves slowly and easily. One person described the way she drives when her rabbit is in the car as: "Driving as if I'm holding a scalding cup of coffee filled to the brim."

Air Travel

Most major airlines will accept rabbits, but you have to tell them ahead of time that you are bringing a live animal for the flight. There are many rules to traveling via air with a rabbit. You must have a proper airline-approved travel cage if you are traveling with the rabbit, and it must be of the type that will fit beneath your seat. Your rabbit must have a current (within 10 days) health certificate signed by your veterinarian. If the weather is above or below certain temperatures, you will not be able to fly the rabbit.

If your rabbit is not flying under the seat with you, it is a good idea to put extra hay in his cage as padding against bumps, serving as something for him to burrow into to avoid drafts and noises if he is traveling as "baggage" and is left out on the tarmac for a while.

It's also a good idea to line the cage well with either newspaper or paper towels to absorb urine. You should affix a day's supply of food and treats to the top of his cage. It is also a good idea to put your name and address on a shipping label other than the one provided by the airline. It's always better to be safe than sorry. Large letters on top of the cage spelling out "Live Animal" can help people on board the plane keep an eye out for mishandling if you are not traveling with your rabbit and he has to fly in the hold of the plane instead of beneath your seat. Be sure your rabbit has something really tasty that will keep him chewing so that the air pressure won't hurt his ears too badly on takeoff and landings.

If you are moving from one location to another, be prepared to do as much as possible to make the new home as much like the old one as possible, at least as far as your rabbit is concerned. Put him in the same cage, in the same situation as in your old home. If you are moving a long distance away, be aware that all rabbit foods are not available all over the country. Either pick up some of the new brand you will be feeding and start slowly switching your rabbit over before you move, or take along a few extra bags of his regular food now to switch over gradually later. (Rabbit food will keep for long periods of time, especially if refrigerated or frozen.) Be sure to keep hay with your rabbit during and after

Part 2

What to Bring When Traveling With Your Rabbit

Proper paperwork: It's a good idea to carry a current health certificate for your rabbit, especially if you are traveling through any state or country borders.

Identification: Be sure your pet has on an ID tag in the unlikely event of his getting a chance to run away. This tag should have your name and a phone number you can be reached at while you're traveling (either a cell phone, your vet's number, or a neighbor who will forward any messages).

Food and water: Always carry a good supply of rabbit food when you travel. Don't count on being able to find your normal brand in other parts of the country. Be sure it's kept in a well-sealed container, and you should feed your rabbit a little less while traveling, due to the possibility of upset stomachs. Plenty of water is also very important, because stress can easily cause a rabbit to become overheated when riding in a car, and he'll crave extra fluids.

Litter Pan: Purchase a small litter pan that will fit in his travel cage.

Toys and Bedding: Take along some of his favorite toys and bedding that he's had in his cage at home. Both will make him feel more secure and help him realize that you are a common denominator in all situations in his life. Wherever *you* are is home.

Photograph: Always keep your rabbit closely confined when you're away from home. Having a lost rabbit is terrible when you're on your home turf, but in strange surroundings, it can create overwhelming problems. Carry a photograph of your pet with you in case he is lost and you have to create "Lost Pet" posters. This can also be used as identification and proof of ownership if he is turned into a shelter.

Lightweight Collar: Keep a lightweight collar on your rabbit at all times during travel, complete with an identification tag and a bell. The bell might help you find him, and the ID tag will help his finder contact you. (Don't include your home phone; remember, you're not home, you're on vacation; instead, use your cell phone, your vet's, a neighbor's, or a relative's phone number.)

the move. Stress may keep a rabbit from eating, but even a rabbit under severe stress will sometimes nibble hay without thinking. This could mean the difference between a sick bunny and a healthy one.

Bunny-Sitters

If it's not imperative that your bunny travels with you, you might want to consider leaving your pet at home in capable hands. You can either ask a reliable friend who knows your bunny and whom your bunny is familiar with, or pay a professional pet-sitter to take care of your furry friend while you are gone.

Whether you ask a friend or hire a professional, you should follow the same guidelines. Be sure you meet with the person well in advance of your travel date to make sure they know what they're getting into. Be certain that they understand that "taking care of my rabbit" doesn't mean popping into your home once a day to fill up a water bottle and drop a cupful of pellets in his food dish. They should understand that you want quality time spent with your rabbit. That includes exercise time, treat time, and "sit together" time.

You should leave a detailed and well-written list of instructions regarding your normal feeding and cleaning routine, and you should make it clear that you don't want them to deviate from this. (Your rabbit will be stressed enough by having "strangers" in the house without having his schedule adjusted.) They should be given the name, phone number, and address of your veterinarian and other people in the area who can give advice on rabbit care in case your vet is unavailable.

You may want to leave your rabbit with a pet-sitter or reliable friend when you travel.

You should leave your credit card information with your veterinarian so, in case of emergency, the pet-sitter doesn't have to worry about how to pay for proper vet care.

It's a very good idea to put daily portions of food, vegetables, and fruits in individual, zipper-topped plastic storage bags, plainly marked as to what each holds, how it is to be fed, how often, and when not to feed. (If your rabbit is exhibiting signs of diarrhea or other intestinal upset, some fruits and vegetables should not be fed.) Most fruits and veggies can be stored in bags in your refrigerator for at least a week.

Boarding

As hard as it may be for you to understand, none of your friends may want to take on the responsibility of taking care of your rabbit while you are traveling. If you can't find a pet-sitter in your area, you will have to either plan to take your rabbit along with you, or find a boarding facility that will accept rabbits.

You should be aware that most boarding facilities won't have the time or facilities to provide your rabbit with all the comforts of home. You may have to be satisfied with knowing that your rabbit is having all of his basic needs met and is with pet professionals who will know what to do in the case of an emergency.

Showing Your Rabbit

If it's a Saturday or Sunday, the chances are quite good that somewhere in the US, rabbit lovers are gathering for a rabbit show. Although dog and cat shows garner a lot of attention and publicity, many people who aren't part of the "rabbit world" are surprised to hear that there are rabbit shows, too. In fact, there are more than 2,500 American Rabbit Breeders Association, Incorporated (ARBA) sanctioned shows, 4-H, and county fairs rabbit shows throughout the US each year.

The ARBA is the only national association that has the authority to sanction rabbit shows in the US. As the only registration entity for rabbits in the US, the ARBA is responsible for not only sanctioning shows, but also for licensing the official judges, maintaining the registration system, and overseeing the standard for all of the 45 rabbit breeds that it recognizes. At this time, there are more than 30,000 members of the ARBA.

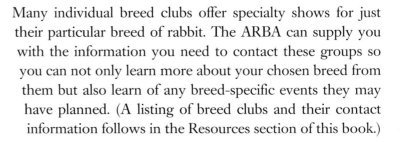

Many individual breed clubs offer specialty shows for just their particular breed of rabbit. The ARBA can supply you with the information you need to contact these groups so you can not only learn more about your chosen breed from them but also learn of any breed-specific events they may have planned. (A listing of breed clubs and their contact information follows in the Resources section of this book.)

Most rabbit shows are daylong events that make for great family fun. Although some exhibitors are serious about their entries of prized show animals, you can show your pet bunny at any rabbit show, even if he's not a purebred, much less registered or show bred. You will have to have your rabbit tattooed for official identification before he can be shown, however. The

Rabbit shows are daylong events that make for great family fun.

tattoo can be anything you choose (letters, numbers, or symbols), but it must be in the left ear.

These tattoos are to distinguish one rabbit from another. While some breeds have markings that make each rabbit unique, some breeds look pretty much the same from one rabbit to another. Without a tattoo to tell them apart, a judge would have a difficult time keeping track of who was who. If you only have one or two rabbits, it would be unlikely for you to get them mixed up, but in rabbitries of hundreds of rabbits that look alike, the tattoo may be the only way breeders can tell their rabbits apart.

There is a fee for entering, but it is usually a minimal amount. All entrants are eligible to compete for prizes ranging from money to ribbons to trophies. The national ARBA convention and rabbit show takes place once a year at different locations around the US and attracts an average of 1,500 exhibitors.

Many individual breed clubs offer specialty shows for their breed of rabbit.

Classes and Standards

Rabbit shows are officially referred to as "rabbit and cavy shows," as there are classes for cavies (guinea pigs) as well. Most shows have classes for adult competitors and for youth competitors, as well as having different classes for different ages and varieties of rabbits within each breed. Each breed has a "Standard of Perfection" that each rabbit is judged against before he actually competes with the other rabbits in his class.

This standard spells out exactly what the rabbit is supposed to look like—exact shape and structure of the head, ears, feet, legs, tail, and body. It describes

What Makes a Judge Worthy of Passing Judgment on MY Bunny?

Before someone can become an ARBA judge, they have to have knowledge of all the rabbit breeds, have experience in breeding and owning rabbits, and pass a written test provided by ARBA regarding every rabbit breed they will be approved to judge. Then they have to apprentice under licensed judges for several shows before they will be allowed to apply for their own license. ARBA has the final say as to who can and cannot become a licensed and approved rabbit judge.

Show rabbits require identification tattoos, shown here.

"Registered" Rabbits

If someone offers you a "registered rabbit," be sure you get proper documentation to prove that claim. Unlike dogs and cats that are "registerable" if both parents are purebred and registered, rabbits cannot be registered by ARBA until they have been individually judged by a certified ARBA judge and deemed purebred and of good quality.

Most purebred baby bunnies that are offered by breeders are sold as "pedigreed;" these will come to you with a three, four, or five-generation pedigree or family tree showing the bunny's ancestors. You cannot receive "registration papers" or a "registration application" as you do with a puppy or kitten. You'll just have to wait until your bunny grows up a little and can be examined by an ARBA judge.

Every breed has a "Standard of Perfection" that each rabbit is judged against.

the type and feel of the fur and all acceptable colors and markings (even including toenail colors on some breeds). Each characteristic is given a certain number of points on the scale of importance. For instance, some breeds may allow 50 points for fur, while others allow only 10, but give a 50-point importance to body shape, etc.

Breed judging is divided into classes based on the sex and age of the rabbit. Some breeds have weight divisions as well. The smaller breeds have fewer class divisions than the larger breeds. Small breeds are divided into senior bucks and senior does (older than six months) and junior bucks and junior does (younger than six months). Larger breeds have an additional class of intermediates for each sex for those six to eight months, and their senior classes are for those animals that are more than eight months of age.

Part 2

The Show Process

Some breeds are also divided into "varieties" if the breed is recognized in several colors. The varieties are divided into the same class types as the breeds.

When rabbits show up at a show site, they are carried into the show building, where they wait their turn before the judge. Once they are at the judging table, they are placed into small "holding cages" while the judge picks up each individual rabbit and examines him carefully. First, any animals that have disqualifications according to their breed standard are removed from judging. The remaining animals are then placed according to the judge's opinion of their quality.

After each class, the first-place winners remain at the judging table. After all the judging of the classes of that breed, each first-place winner is judged against the others of his breed, and the animal that the judge believes most closely meets the qualifications set in the breed standard for that breed will be named the Best of Breed. The Best Opposite Sex winner is then selected from class winners of the sex opposite to the sex of the rabbit named Best of Breed.

At the end of the day, each Best of Breed winner goes back into competition for the selection of the Best in Show rabbit. That rabbit is the one that the judge believes best meets his breed's Standard of Perfection.

Besides being a competitive event, it's also a shopper's paradise for rabbit lovers, with vendor booths set up with rabbit supplies, clothing, and household goods decorated with rabbit motifs, and of course, good food!

Although rabbit shows are very competitive and a showcase for getting "bragging rights" for breeding

What Can I Win, Johnny?

No one is going to get rich from rabbit show winnings. Most prizes are trophies and ribbons. The biggest gain in showing rabbits is the points they are competing to win to work toward a title of "Grand Champion" from ARBA. If a rabbit wins first place against five rabbits owned by three different owners, that rabbit wins a "leg." If an ARBA registered rabbit wins three legs in at least three shows judged by at least two different judges, he is eligible to apply for Grand Champion status from ARBA.

Each Best of Breed winner competes for the title of Best in Show.

Show rabbits require careful grooming and preparation.

quality animals, rabbit shows are first and foremost social events where people who share a love for rabbits gather and discuss their interest. Winning trophies, points, honors, and even some money can never equal the companionship aspect of a rabbit show.

Getting Ready To Show

Getting ready for a rabbit show means far more than deciding what to wear and how to pack your car to get the most space for rabbits and their paraphernalia. Getting ready for a show starts weeks before the show date by grooming your rabbits carefully, maintaining good socialization practices with them, training them to pose for judging, and making sure their weight stays within the standard.

You should spend the day before the show making sure that all your carry cages and equipment are clean and presentable. Never show up at a rabbit show with dirty cages. You should also be certain you carry everything with you to keep both you and your rabbits comfortable during the long judging day ahead. This means a lawn chair, cool drinks, and something good to read during slow times for you, and hay, water, and a few treats for your bunnies.

How Do I Find A Show?

If you join ARBA, you will receive a copy of their *Domestic Rabbits* magazine every other month. In that magazine is a listing of upcoming shows and the contact person for each show.

You can also find show information by going to the official ARBA website at http://www.arba.net/. There are "open shows" that are open to exhibitors of all ages or "youth shows" that accept entries only from youths less than 19 years of age.

Remember the old adage "It's not whether you win or lose, it's how you play the game." You have paid for that judge's opinion on that day. Don't argue with his or her decision. Accept it gracefully and hope that the next judge you have sees in your rabbit what you see when you look at him. No two people will interpret a breed standard in exactly the same way.

Part Three
Your Rabbit's Health

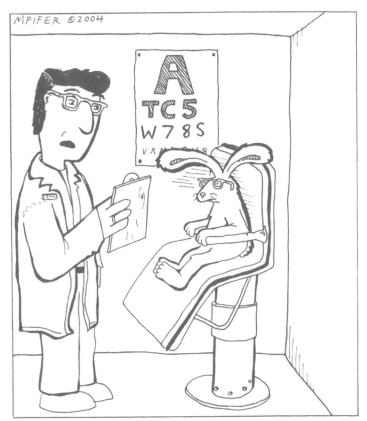

"Your eyesight is terrible! I feel strange for asking, but are you eating enough carrots?"

General Health Care

A healthy rabbit is a happy rabbit, and a happy rabbit makes for a happy owner! Most breeds of rabbits will remain quite healthy if they receive adequate daily care and attention. Even healthy rabbits can get sick, however, so it is up to you as a loving, caring pet owner to watch for symptoms of illness or the need for emergency vet care.

A healthy rabbit's coat should be glossy with no bare patches. The eyes should be bright with no watery discharge, the ears should be clean, and the mouth should not have signs of excessive saliva. A healthy rabbit should be alert and should move freely without any obvious pain or stiffness. The feet and nose should also be clean, with no

Healthy rabbits should have a glossy coat, bright eyes, and clean ears.

Knowing your rabbit's normal routine will help you detect illness.

obvious sores, and the nails should not be overgrown.

Detecting Health Problems Early On

Finding most health problems in their early stages means that they will be more easily treatable and that the chances of a complete cure are much better. Unfortunately, because of the rabbit's evolutionary history as prey animals where almost every other animal in the food chain is their natural predator, rabbits are extremely stoic when they are in pain or suffering from an illness. Predators in the wild will zone in on any animal that acts sick or weak, knowing that those animals will be easier prey than their healthy counterparts. Therefore, sick rabbits throughout history have developed an inborn tendency not to show these outward signs of illness, which would make them more likely to be dinner for some savvy predator.

Although this evolutionary trait is a marvel to humans, it makes it very hard to tell for sure when our house rabbits are sick. Even though there is no predator to take advantage of their illness, most rabbits will still pretend to feel fine and literally suffer in silence. This means that it takes a very attentive owner to notice the first signs of his or her rabbit feeling sick. However, knowing your rabbit's normal routine is the best way to ensure his survival should something go wrong–this way, you'll recognize the first signs of changes that could indicate illness.

Sometimes these first signs may be something as elusive as a slight change in the way your bunny hops, what part of the cage he sits in, or what treats he will eat or turn down. Perhaps he isn't playing with his favorite toy, or his food dish still has food long after it is usually empty. Maybe his water bottle doesn't need filling as often as it usually does. While none of these things constitutes a middle-of-the-night emergency call to the vet, these symptoms are causes for concern. Most likely you should schedule a trip to the veterinarian for a checkup to be sure nothing is wrong.

Taking Your Rabbit's Temperature

One of the first things to do when you suspect that your rabbit may be sick is to take his temperature. If you do not know how to do this, have your vet show you. Always use a plastic thermometer to eliminate the danger of the thermometer breaking off while you are taking his temperature.

You should first take your rabbit's temperature when you know he is *not* sick or stressed to get a baseline body temperature for him. Then you will have something to go by when you think he is sick and could be running a fever.

Normal rabbit body temperature ranges between 101°F–103°F (38.3°C–39.4°C). A slightly elevated temperature (around 104°F/39.9°C) can occur due to emotional stress, heat stress, or the early stages of an infection. A very high temperature (105°F/40.5°C or higher) should be considered an emergency. Lifesaving cooling measures (ice packs, room temperature subcutaneous fluids, application of rubbing alcohol to the ears) should be begun even before you leave for the veterinarian's office.

If the body temperature remains at 106°F/41.1°C or higher for any length of time, irreversible brain damage can occur, even if the bunny otherwise survives the ordeal. You should never immerse your rabbit in cold water under any circumstances. The shock of being in water, as well as the sudden coldness, can send him into convulsions and can cause a fatal shock to his system.

A temperature lower than normal is of equal concern in a rabbit. Abnormally low body temperature can signify shock or a systemic

Rabbits instinctively conceal signs of illness.

The temperature of a healthy rabbit ranges between 101°F and 103°F.

infection. Bacteria in the bloodstream, in the case of a systemic infection, will use up so much of the rabbit's glucose (blood sugar) that he will not be able to maintain a normal body temperature. This must be treated immediately and aggressively, sometimes with intravenous antibiotics and sugar solution, which must be administered by your veterinarian.

A temperature lower than 100°F is always to be considered a rabbit emergency. The bunny should be wrapped in towels warm from the dryer or with a wrapped hot-water bottle on the way to the emergency vet. If you don't have a hot water bottle, take a zipper-top plastic freezer bag and fill it with hot water or heat it in the microwave. Wrap the bag in a tea towel and place it against your bunny. Putting plastic soda bottles of hot water in his travel cage will also keep the cage warm for him. If you use a heating pad, be sure it is turned on low and has a nice thick cover to avoid burning his tender skin.

Common Rabbit Health Problems

Most rabbits can remain in good health with proper care, nutrition, and attention. However, illness can affect even the most well-cared-for rabbit, and the following section outlines some of the common medical problems rabbits suffer from so that you can recognize the symptoms of these illnesses should they affect your pet. Always see your veterinarian if you suspect a problem.

Wool Block

Wool block is to a rabbit what a hairball is to a cat. Because bunnies groom themselves as often as cats do, and because they ingest their dead wool in the same way that cats ingest their dead hairs, the wool can ball up in their stomachs. Unlike cats, however, this situation can easily be fatal for a rabbit.

To prevent wool block, carefully groom rabbit breeds that molt.

Symptoms of wool block are not always easily detectable. You might notice that your rabbit isn't eating as much, or you might notice a lot of wool in his droppings. Some of his droppings might even appear to be woven together with strings of wool. (Some breeders refer to this as "pearl necklace droppings.") Over time, his droppings will get smaller and smaller as the impaction increases in size.

A bunny that is molting is most likely to get an impaction or wool blockage. Therefore, it is very important to keep your bunny either plucked or shorn during his molts. Bunnies molt about every three months. Every second molt is light, followed by a heavier molt. It is usually during this heavy molt that the greatest risk of wool block occurs.

Treatment

Fresh pineapple (not canned) or papaya can break down food in a rabbit's stomach, enabling the wool to pass through more easily. Giving papaya tablets (usually found in human health-food stores) can be used as a preventative but is rarely successful as a treatment after the problem has occurred. Feeding the woody part of a pineapple core to your rabbit can not only prevent the problem, but sometimes can be used successfully once the impaction has started.

Hairball remedies for cats can be effective for rabbits fighting wool block as well. Some rabbits especially like the malt-flavored ones. Just don't use them at the same time that you are using a pineapple or papaya treatment or preventative, as they will fight against each other and eventually cancel out each other's effectiveness. Some breeders report having success by alternating the treatments in 8- to 10-hour intervals throughout the day. Sometimes putting a dab of petroleum jelly on your rabbit's nose can be effective, as he will rub his nose with his paws, then lick his paws clean, which gets the jelly into the stomach, where it can help smooth the way for the impaction to move. It is important to stop trying home remedies if you're not seeing 100-percent improvement within 72 hours. At that point, it's time to call out the big guns for the situation and take the rabbit to visit your veterinarian.

Snuffles

Although the term "snuffles" sounds cute and charming, when your vet returns that verdict after examining your very sick rabbit, it definitely loses its charm. Colds among rabbits are known as "snuffles." Typical snuffles will clear up easily with proper treatment from your veterinarian and won't return if the rabbit is kept in clean, dry, draft-free living quarters. Some rabbits seem prone to getting snuffles again and again, no matter how cozy and clean their houses are kept. This leads many rabbit professionals to believe that different

Part 3

irritants may indeed cause snuffles and colds. Whatever causes snuffles, a wet nose is usually the first indication that your rabbit has caught a cold.

Eye Problems

Any time you notice any changes in your rabbit's eyes or the amount of tears he is producing, it is time for a vet visit. You should check the white of the eye for any color changes or persistent redness. Watch for color changes in the iris, irregular edges to the pupil, or any clouding of the cornea. Cancer of the eye happens fairly often in rabbits, and as with any type of cancer, early detection is the key to successful treatment. You may choose to see or be referred to a veterinary ophthalmologist, who specializes in the eyes of all animal species and is able to provide more specialized care for complex problems. Yes, it will be more expensive, but your rabbit's vision may depend on it. Don't delay, as eye conditions can be quite painful or cause permanent damage, leading to blindness.

Even rabbits kept in clean, cozy environments can get snuffles.

Eye Discharge

A rabbit's eyes are very sensitive. If they begin to exhibit signs of a discharge, your rabbit should go to your veterinarian for a checkup. Runny eyes are usually a symptom of a bacterial infection. It is important that treatment begin as soon as possible to keep the infection from spreading to the rabbit's jaw or respiratory tract, which may represent a very dangerous medical situation for your bunny. A rabbit that has an abscess in a jaw can also have excessive tearing or other discharge from his eyes.

A rabbit's eyes can also water more than normal due to an obstruction or inflammatory debris in the tear duct instead of from a bacterial infection. This duct is a passage for tears between the eye and the nose. If it is blocked, the drainage of tears will overflow onto the cheeks. If a blockage is causing the discharge, your veterinarian can easily flush this duct to remove the debris. After such a problem, you should keep a close watch on your bunny, as you may find he will be prone to this problem from now on.

Conjunctivitis

Rabbits often suffer from conjunctivitis or "pinkeye," an inflammation of the membrane inside the eyelid. Pinkeye in the rabbit can be very nasty, is contagious, and commonly recurs. Symptoms include excessive tearing, reddened and/or crusty mucous membranes of the eye, and clouding of the pupil. Contributing factors can include allergies, stress, excessive dust, and constant exposure to sunlight. Flies are known carriers of pinkeye.

If your rabbit will let you, hold a moist, warm cloth against the affected eye for a few minutes. Do this as often as your pet seems to need or want it the first day, then once or twice a day after that until the condition improves. If it hasn't cleared up in a few days, you should call your veterinarian. If your rabbit is keeping

Take your rabbit to the vet if you notice any eye changes.

his eye closed or if he won't let you touch the eye at all, take him to your veterinarian immediately. There are many broad-spectrum antibiotic ophthalmic powders and ointments available for treatment, and these should be continued long after symptoms have disappeared. Consult a veterinarian regarding the preferred products and treatment.

Dacryocystitis

Disease of the tear duct or the lacrimal sac is called dacryocystitis. It is most often secondary to bacterial infections that occur within the duct. It can be treated with the correct antibiotics, but always be sure that any veterinarian who prescribes antibiotics is a rabbit professional, as some antibiotics are not tolerated by a rabbit's system and can prove fatal. Never give your rabbit amoxicillin, even if a veterinarian prescribes it. (Amoxicillin is usually given in a pink liquid form that smells rather like bubble gum.) In fact, any antibiotic that ends in "-cillin" is likely going to do more harm than good for your rabbit. Instead, find a veterinarian who will prescribe more rabbit-friendly antibiotics, such as Chloramphenicol; Tetracycline; enrofloxins, such as Baytril or Cipro; or sulfa-based drugs, like Septra or TMS.

Misshapen Eyelids

A misshapen eyelid can also cause excessive tearing. There is a congenital condition known as entropion, in which the eyelid folds under, allowing the eyelashes to continually

A rabbit's eyes are sensitive, so make sure to protect them from harmful elements.

Part 3

rub the eyeball, causing painful corneal ulcerations. Your vet can either do the surgery to correct this problem or refer you to a rabbit surgeon. Sometimes a rabbit's eyelids will simply fold incorrectly, without letting the eyelashes rub the eye but still causing enough friction to create excess tearing.

Allergies

Rabbits' eye problems can also stem from allergies. Have you changed the litter or bedding? Cleaned with a different disinfectant? Fed new foods? Sometimes a rabbit can get watery eyes as a result of an allergic reaction to the dust in his hay or litter. Some wood shavings put off volatile gases that can irritate a bunny's sensitive eyes. If possible, go back to whatever you were doing originally and see if the problem clears up on its own. If it doesn't, a trip to the vet is in order.

Tear Stains

Before the tears have a chance to stain your rabbit's coat, you can use a bit of saline solution (used for humans' contact lenses) on your bunny's cheeks to crystallize the tears so that you can brush them from his coat. You may find that if your rabbit has a chronic problem with eye discharge, the fur on his cheek may peel off from the constant moistness, called "tear scald" (much like a baby's diaper rash). For lesions on the cheek, apply a dab of topical anesthetic powder to absorb the moisture and prompt healing. Just be sure to keep the powder itself away from the eyes.

Dry Eyes

A dry eye can be as dangerous, or perhaps even more so, than an eye that is overtearing. Without enough tears remaining on the eye's surface to keep it adequately moist, the cornea is more easily subject to scratches. Oddly enough, discharge from the eyes may be a signal that your rabbit's eyes are too dry. Discharge is a symptom of corneal ulcerations that have occurred when the bunny's eyes were not kept moist enough. If this problem persists, you may have to put drops in his eyes on a regular basis to ensure proper moistness.

Notice the Norm

Any change in normal behavior may indicate an underlying health problem. Notify your veterinarian if you notice your rabbit:

- Is eating or drinking less than normal
- Is being either restless or lethargic—or having a crouched or huddled appearance
- Has a coat that looks dull or is soiled or itchy
- Has a discharge from the eyes, ears, or nose
- Is soiling himself around the genital area with either urine or feces
- Has feces that are abnormal in color or texture
- Is producing more urine or less urine–or urine that is unusual in color
- Has an offensive odor from the ears, mouth, or vent
- Is grinding his teeth loudly
- Is having difficulty eating, drinking, or moving around
- Is having difficulty in breathing or is emitting raspy noises from the chest

Any of these can be symptoms of a serious, life-threatening health problem. Set up an appointment with your veterinarian right away.

Dental Problems and Treatment

Although your rabbit won't have to make regular trips to a dentist, brush after meals, or learn to use dental floss, you will have to learn to help him take care of his teeth. Because so much of a rabbit's life is spent chewing, he is "designed" to have teeth that grow continuously throughout his life. It is imperative that you supply your rabbit with tough objects to chew on to keep his teeth filed down naturally. Sticks (rabbits love limbs from apple trees, especially) or pieces of wood (make sure the wood is untreated and therefore safe for ingestion) make excellent chew toys. You can also purchase specially treated wooden pieces that have different shapes, scents, and tastes.

If a rabbit's teeth are properly aligned, you will find that chewing wooden pieces is all that is necessary to keep teeth in good shape. However, just like humans, all bunny teeth are not created equal. Some rabbits have crooked or "maloccluded" bites that are not aligned in a correct manner so that they will wear down properly. These rabbits will have to make

Rabbits need to chew on rough objects to keep their teeth filed down naturally.

Part 3

regular trips to the vet to have their teeth properly filed down. Under no circumstances should you follow the directions of "old timers" who will tell you just to use nail clippers to nip off the tips of your rabbit's teeth. This opens up the central nerve to infection that will be painful, if not fatal, for your bunny. Maloccluded teeth that are not filed correctly can keep your rabbit from being able to chew his food properly, which can cause digestive problems. In severe cases, the rabbit may not be able to eat at all and can literally starve to death.

Diarrhea

Diarrhea in rabbits, as it is in small human children, can be fatal. Always take your rabbit to a veterinarian immediately if you see signs of diarrhea. There are different levels of diarrhea in rabbits. The most visible is, of course, runny, smelly, and messy. It is also considered diarrhea if the pellets appear normal but will squash flat if you touch or attempt to sweep them up. You may also see pellets that clump together. Any of these types of diarrhea are reason to make an appointment with your veterinarian. Be sure to notice and be able to tell your vet if your rabbit's stomach is rumbling or growling and if there have been any very small or misshapen droppings as well.

Ear Problems

A rabbit's ears are the most sensitive part of his body. Although they range in size from barely visible to so long that the bunny steps on them when trying to walk, all rabbits can suffer the same types of ear maladies.

The Ears Have It

While mites, infections, and wax accumulations do not constitute an emergency, not taking care of them can certainly put your pet's life in danger and rapidly cause an emergency situation.

Ear canker, or ear mange, is caused when a mite chews the skin on the side of the ear, causing irritation, redness, and soreness. A whitish to tan crusty material develops in the ear. Treatment for ear canker consists of swabbing the ears (inside and out, although not deep into the ear canal) as well as the head and neck area with mineral oil or ear mite medication.

Ear Mites

Your vet can take a gentle scraping from your pet's ear, and by looking under a microscope, see if any mites are present. Usually, mites will prove their presence by leaving an accumulation of a dark residue in the ear. Although they're extremely pesky little critters and can cause your rabbit a lot of discomfort, they can be easily gotten rid of with an injectable or topical veterinary preparation. Be wary of over-the-counter ear mite treatments, as some of them can do more harm than good and can even exacerbate the situation.

Ear Infections

An inner ear infection may start with an outer ear infection that remains unnoticed and untreated until it gradually works its way into the inner ear. A middle ear infection can result from an upper respiratory infection or from bacteria in the nasal cavity or the bloodstream. Treatment of a severe ear infection may have to be aggressive to get rid of it completely. Your vet may want to do a culture to see exactly what bacteria is present and what antibiotic(s) would treat it the most efficiently. If the infection is not severe, he or she may decide to treat it initially with one of the antibiotics known to be usually successful in curing ear infections. If you don't see any improvement within a few weeks, further testing and a change in antibiotic will be necessary.

Earwax Accumulation

Wax builds up in a healthy rabbit's ear on a regular basis. It can be lifted out easily with a cotton swab–just be very careful not to push the wax farther down into the ear canal, and don't wait until the buildup has become severe. You might want to consider softening the

Ears are the most sensitive parts on a rabbit's body.

Wax needs to be cleaned out of your rabbit's ears on a regular basis.

Part 3

wax before you try to remove it. You can use a mild ear cleaner containing Chlorhexidine. Squirt a few drops into the ear and massage around the outer ear base to spread the drops throughout the ear; then remove the wax with the swab. Because a rabbit's ears are the most sensitive part of the body, the rabbit may not like this treatment, as it tickles and feels strange to him. Normal earwax is not to be confused with the waxy residue left behind by ear mites.

Bladder Disease

Although most people will rush their rabbit to the vet at the first sign of red urine, it takes a more observant pet owner to see the true signs of bladder disease or infection in his or her rabbit. Although signs of trouble vary from rabbit to rabbit, you should seek veterinary help if you see your rabbit straining but not producing any urine or see him hopping in and out of his litter pan more often than usual. Wetness around the genital area, urine scald on the lower belly and around the genitals, or dribbling without any control is an obvious warning sign that should not be ignored. By the time your rabbit becomes lethargic or anorectic, it may be too late to get help. It's better to be safe than sorry.

Red urine normally occurs when a rabbit eats vegetables with beta-carotene.

Red Urine

A rabbit's normal urine will vary in color, ranging from clear to yellow to brown to bright red. Although many pets are rushed to their vets when their rabbits produce red urine, telling their vet that they see blood in the urine, this usually isn't really the case and isn't usually a cause for alarm. Blood in the urine, from either a vaginal or urinary tract infection, is almost impossible to see with the naked eye and is usually found by a veterinarian after running tests. Thus, red urine actually does not always indicate blood is present. If you want to double check that it is indeed blood you are seeing in your rabbit's urine, you can test it by using a urine "dipstick," which can be purchased over the counter from a pharmacy.

It is believed that the red in a rabbit's urine is from plant pigmentation and rarely from blood and does not affect the health of the animal. The color usually returns to normal in a matter of a few days, although it make take as long as three to four weeks for it to completely go away. Red urine may occur when a rabbit is on antibiotics, when the weather first turns cold in the fall, and after the rabbit eats fir leaves, carrots, spinach, or other vegetables that contain beta-carotene. Unless you see your rabbit straining to urinate with no results or see faint pink tinges in normal yellow or clear urine, there is likely no need for a veterinary visit.

GI Stasis

A rabbit's intestines are very tricky and intricate. If they become static and stop digesting, a situation known as GI Stasis takes place, which can be dangerous if not fatal for your rabbit. This can be caused by stress, dehydration, pain from an illness or disorder (such as a sore tooth, gas, urinary tract infection, etc.), an intestinal blockage, or insufficient dietary fiber (the reason that giving hay is so important!).

Left untreated by a veterinarian, this slowdown of normal intestinal movement can result in a very painful death for your rabbit. If your rabbit doesn't eat for 12 hours or stops producing fecal matter, you should consider it an emergency and seek medical care for him as soon as possible.

Treatment for GI Stasis

Although *E. lactobacillus acidophilus* is not normally present in a rabbit's intestines, many breeders and veterinarians have found that a good dose of dried *Lactobacillus* (available at health food stores in either a powder or capsule form) seems to help a rabbit survive a GI Stasis episode until the intestine starts moving again. No one seems to know why it works, but most who have tried it agree that it does. Do not use yogurt instead of the powder; the milk, sugars, and carbohydrates in yogurt can actually exacerbate the existing problem by promoting harmful bacterial overgrowth.

Once your bunny is on the road to recovery, it's time to put on your thinking cap and decide what caused the problem in the first place. Does your rabbit get sufficient fiber in his diet? Are you giving him too many nutritionally incorrect treats? Does he have an underlying infection, illness, or environmental problem that's causing him enough stress to shut down his intestines? Does he have overgrown molars, an abscessed tooth, or a maloccluded bite that does not allow him to chew his food completely?

Part 3

Remember that GI Stasis is often a symptom of an underlying problem, a red flag that something else is terribly wrong in your rabbit's system. Once he has recovered from this episode, it's time to allow your vet to do some blood workups and other testing to see if another health problem is lurking.

Bacterial Infections

The first indication of a bacterial infection can be a runny nose or eyes or perhaps a faint rattling of the chest that you can hear if you put your head against your rabbit's side. In rare instances, you may hear your rabbit cough. In any case, it is very important that you take your rabbit to the vet at the first sign of an infection appear. Caught early enough, most infections can be cured. Your veterinarian will do a culture to see what bacteria your rabbit is fighting and what antibiotic would be the most effective.

The *Pasteurella* bacterium is the most common in the home environment. Cats can carry this bacterium in their mouths. The most common signs that *Pasteurella* bacteria are present are respiratory problems, eye or nose discharge, and head tilt. This is very contagious, being easily transmitted from one rabbit to another. Many rabbits are carriers of these bacteria and can live a full life span without complications. Some rabbits may show symptoms while under stress.

Make sure the temperature is cool and constant when you take your rabbit outdoors.

Overheating

Rabbits do not deal well with excess heat. Remember, in their natural habitat, they live in burrows deep in the earth where the temperatures remain cool and constant. You should be sure that your rabbit's cage is not in direct sunlight. In hot summer months, you can place a frozen bottle of water in his cage so he always has a cool place to lie down. You can also put a ceramic or marble tile in his cage to keep him cool as well. You should feed him lots of chilled vegetables during hot weather; he can use the extra liquids he'll get from them, as well as the coolness. Never take your rabbit outdoors during the hottest part of the day, but keep him inside in a climate-controlled area.

Pumpkin-Pellet Energy Food

If your bunny is recuperating from an illness and is too weak to eat solid foods, many breeders swear by the following recipe that can be fed through a syringe to really debilitated bunnies.

1 large can pumpkin pie filling (no sugar or spices added)

1 tbs banana baby food

1 tbs rabbit food pellets, ground finely in food processor or coffee grinder

pinch of acidophilus powder

Mix well, and refrigerate after mixing. You can force feed four times a day by using a syringe. Instead of using banana baby food, you can mash up half of a banana instead. As the rabbit grows stronger, you can begin to feed in a dish or from a spoon and without grinding the pellets quite so finely.

If you think your rabbit may be suffering from heat stroke, immediately take a cool (not cold) damp cloth and gently rub your rabbit's ears. Never submerse a rabbit in cold water. Keeping his ears cool and damp is an excellent treatment for heat stress. Because they don't sweat like humans or pant like dogs, they lose heat through their ears. Signs of heat stroke include lethargy, difficulty breathing, heavy panting, and loss of appetite.

Parasites

There are many internal and external parasites that can plague rabbits. The most common usually found in house rabbits include ringworm, mites, fleas, ticks, coccidiosis, roundworms, and tapeworms. The signs of parasites can be numerous, from loss of condition and weight to diarrhea or sore skin, depending on the type of parasite and the place of infestation. You should always seek veterinary advice for identification of the parasite and the proper treatment.

Ear Mites

Ear mites are small parasites that produce itchy debris and inflammation in the ear. Ear mites are not visible to the naked eye but can be seen during a veterinary examination. If the parasite is left untreated, the rabbit may inflict wounds to his ear due to scratching or shaking his head. Ear mites are easily treated by your veterinarian with medication you can continue using at home to prevent a reinfestation.

Part 3

Check for fleas when you brush your rabbit's fur.

Fur Mites

Fur mites usually occur on the back between the shoulder blades and look like flaky dandruff. Severe cases may cause hair loss.

Fleas

Fleas are not usually common on pet rabbits. A rabbit may, however, get fleas from other household pets. Treatment consists of using a kitten-safe flea treatment provided by your veterinarian. A flea comb may be used to remove the adult fleas from your rabbit. The rabbit's environment should also be treated for fleas.

Tapeworms

If your rabbit has fleas, he will likely also have tapeworms. If your bunny chews at an itchy place caused by a fleabite and ingests the flea, a tapeworm grows and multiplies. These invisible parasites can make your rabbit very sick if they are not taken care of with treatment by your veterinarian. Your veterinarian can give you medication to treat your rabbit for tapeworms if you see signs of them in his fecal pellets.

Ticks

Although ticks do not usually bother pet rabbits, they may be brought to the house rabbit by other house pets that go outside. Your veterinarian can suggest the best way to rid your rabbit of ticks should you realize you have a problem.

If at some point you do find a tick attached to his skin, don't panic. Using small tweezers, gently grasp the tick and tug very gently until the tick lets go. Do not squeeze! Drop the tick into a small bottle with a tight cap and include the date, so that in case problems arise, the tick can be tested to see if it is the culprit. Wash the tick bite area with soap and water and add an antiseptic. Be sure to sterilize the tweezers as well.

Checking for Parasites

You don't have to take your rabbit to the veterinarian to have him checked for internal parasites or worms. Just take some fresh pellets with you in a zipper-top plastic bag or other glass or plastic container. He or she can do a flotation to check for parasites and send you home with the proper medication for whatever parasites, if any, that he or she finds in the sample.

Coccidia

Coccidia are internal parasites that affect the liver or intestine. Usually only young or stressed rabbits are affected. Signs may include diarrhea, lethargy, weight loss, or poor weight gain. Coccidia can only be diagnosed after a fecal examination by your veterinarian and should be treated only on the recommendation of your vet.

Ringworm

Ringworm is a relatively uncommon but very irritating fungal disease in rabbits. It is caused by an agent similar to the one that causes athlete's foot in people. It is transmitted easily by direct contact with fungal spores on coat, bedding, and soil. It most commonly affects juvenile rabbits and adult rabbits that are under some sort of stress. Ringworm usually causes multiple hairless areas with slightly reddened skin.

These hairless areas are often covered with a slight or heavy crust. The patches usually occur on the head, ears, and forelimbs. Spot applications of topical preparations can be used to treat a few individual areas, but oral medication is required if ringworm affects much of the body. Ringworm is contagious to humans, so care must be exercised when treating it. Be sure to wash your hands well after coming in contact with any rabbit with symptoms of ringworm.

Spay/Neuter—It's the Right Thing to Do

Avoiding unwanted rabbit litters isn't the only reason to have your pet spayed or neutered. By doing so, you will be ensuring your pet a much healthier and happier life! If you're concerned about the risks involved with surgery, you should know that the risks of your rabbit getting a severe health problem later are far greater if you do not have the surgery than if you do. The House Rabbit Society reports that it has had more than 1,000 rabbits spayed or neutered, with only a 0.1-percent (that's "point one," not even one full percent) mortality rate due to anesthesia. Because the risk of reproductive cancer (always fatal) for an unspayed female is approximately 85 percent, you can do the math as to which is actually the best thing for you to do for your rabbit.

While a male rabbit's chances for testicular cancer obviously increase if he is not neutered, the main reason for neutering him will be for behavioral issues. Neutering will eliminate spraying and hormone-related aggression problems. If you choose a rabbit vet with experience in administering anesthesia and doing surgery on rabbits, you should be able to have your rabbit sterilized with a minimal risk.

Part 3

Neutering and Spaying Rabbits

The word "neuter" actually refers to the removal of the reproductive organs of either a male or a female of a species, although people frequently refer to the surgery in only the male as a "neuter" and in the female as a "spay." The scientific terminology for neutering in the male is castration and in the female is ovariohysterectomy.

While prevention of pregnancy is the most common reason to spay or neuter a rabbit, there are many other valid reasons to have your pet sterilized. There are certainly enough rabbits being produced by professional breeders to more than satisfy the pet rabbit market, so if your only reason for wanting to breed a litter is to create pets, you should do your homework. Not only will your pet be happier, but he will also be healthier and will most certainly live longer if he is sterilized at an early age.

Neutering/Spaying and the Prevention of Diseases

The most important reason to spay a female rabbit is that uterine cancer will affect more than 85 percent of all unspayed female rabbits. Uterine cancer is usually not treatable and can rapidly spread to other organs of the body such as the liver, lungs, and the skin, and it is never treatable once it has reached that point. Because rabbits younger than the age of two rarely develop this disease, it is very important to have your female bunny spayed before this age.

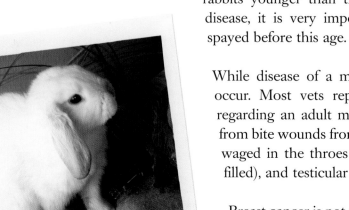
Spaying and neutering can help prevent disease.

While disease of a male rabbit's testicles is rare, it can occur. Most vets report that the problems they treat regarding an adult male's testicles are abscesses (usually from bite wounds from another rabbit, most likely a battle waged in the throes of hormones), hematomas (blood-filled), and testicular cancers.

Breast cancer is not common in female rabbits, but when it occurs, it can spread rapidly and be very difficult to treat. Another common mammary gland disease is mammary dysplasia or cystic mammary glands. This is a benign condition where the mammary glands fill with a cystic material. However, though not fatal, it is very uncomfortable to the pet. Neutering a female rabbit before two years of age will prevent mammary cancer, mammary dysplasia, and cystic mammary glands.

Cancer isn't the only uterine disease that attacks and kills female rabbits. Pyometra (infection of the uterus), uterine aneurism (uterus filled with blood), and endometritis (inflamed uterine lining) are seen by most vets on a regular basis in their unspayed rabbit clients. As with cancer, this is rarely seen in female rabbits younger than two years of age.

Prevention of Behavioral Problems

Neutering doesn't just help you avoid health problems with your rabbit. Even if your female rabbit manages to escape a disease of her "female parts," being unspayed can cause emotional and behavioral problems. Many go into a hormonal state triggered by overactive ovaries that insist that the rabbit is pregnant even if she has not been near a male rabbit. It's easy to believe that the rabbit is indeed about to become a mother as she begins nesting, produces milk, and begins an aggressive protection of her cage and other space.

This aggression will be taken out on her owners and her cage mates and will make her very difficult to handle. Many rabbits that have a false pregnancy will have gastrointestinal disturbances as a result of overeating as she would if she were nurturing a uterus full of embryos. Because there are indeed no embryos to absorb the nutrition from the extra food, the female rabbit's entire system can be disturbed. The stress from this false pregnancy can be very difficult on everyone involved, including the rabbit herself, as she readies herself for babies that never arrive.

Both male and female rabbits can exhibit aggressive behavior when they reach sexual maturity. Rabbits that were sweet, gentle, adorable baby bunnies can

> *Male or Female?*
>
> There is no difference in the health care between male and female rabbits. How do you tell the difference in the sexes? Even at a very early age, a male rabbit will have a greater distance between his anus and his genitals than the female rabbit does.

Part 3

Many behavioral problems can be prevented by spaying and neutering.

Sick Bunny Tips

- Don't take your bunny to the vet any more often than necessary. The stress of travel can slow the recovery of most rabbits. Contact your veterinarian regularly to report on progress and changes. Follow his or her instructions exactly, and if he or she feels the need to see the rabbit, do all you can to make the travel as stress-free as possible (no loud radio, no sudden curves, avoid as many bumps in the road as possible, as well as sudden stops and starts).

- Never separate your sick bunny from his bonded partner. If the problem is contagious, the chances are that his cage partner was exposed at the same time he was, so further exposure can do little harm, but separating them can be quite detrimental to his health.

- Purchase a stethoscope so you can make informed reports to your veterinarian as to heart rates and intestinal gurgling.

- Don't handle your rabbit more often than usual. Although it is our nature to want to nurture an ailing pet, they are usually better off allowed to recuperate in peace. Don't abandon him, and let him know that you care with gentle caresses and tempting treats (if he is allowed to eat), but don't force any attention on him until he's feeling his old self again.

- A rabbit with a temperature lower than 100°F or higher than 103°F is a very sick bunny that should see a veterinarian immediately.

become extremely aggressive when they approach puberty. Suddenly, they don't want to be touched, picked up, or handled in any way. They regress to no longer being litter box trained. They may nip or scratch you. Spaying or neutering at an early age will keep this behavior to a minimum.

Both male and female rabbits spray their urine to mark their territory. If your rabbit is not neutered, this behavior will just continue to escalate as he matures, to the point where housetraining may become impossible. Because the urine of a sexually mature male can have a very unpleasant, pungent odor, this behavior can make it impossible to continue sharing your home with him. Neutering him later on will usually have little or no effect on his spraying. However, neutering at an early age will diminish, if not totally eliminate, this desire to spray everything he comes in contact with.

The Age to Neuter

The best age to neuter is just after sexual maturity. Depending on the breed, this could range from four to six months, and with giant breeds up to possibly nine months. Your breeder or your vet can help you decide if your rabbit is ready to be neutered. You should note that if the rabbit is neutered much younger than four months of age, not only is the surgery more difficult due to the immature condition of the reproductive organs (in males, both testicles may not even be descended into the scrotal sacs yet), but we also do not know what the long-term effect is on the endocrine system of the body. To be sure that your rabbit reaches his correct height, weight, and body and bone mass, wait until he has reached sexual maturity (but not too long afterward) before you schedule his surgery.

The best age to neuter is just after sexual maturity.

In Case of Emergency

Because there is no 911 to call for bunnies, it's best to know how to recognize the difference between a routine medical problem and a true emergency so that you can deal with either situation should it occur. As always, the best preparation you can have is to always pay attention to your rabbit's normal behaviors, habits, and conditions. This way, you will recognize any abnormalities that could signal a problem.

The information in this chapter isn't intended to take the place of a veterinary visit for diagnosis or treatment, but it certainly can save your bunny's life until he receives proper care from a professional.

The best emergency preparation is to pay attention to your rabbit's normal behaviors.

When to Prepare

The time to make preparations for an emergency is while your rabbit is happy and healthy. You can pretty well count on an emergency occurring at some time during your rabbit's life. Make sure you have not only chosen the right vet and a good backup vet, but also that you know both of those vets' schedules! Some vets work only a few days a week or work later on some days. Knowing when they're there can come in handy when you're dealing with an emergency and want to find a veterinarian fast.

Keep the names, addresses, and phone numbers of your vet, your backup vet, and an emergency clinic beside your telephone. If any of your vets have an office in an area with which you are unfamiliar, go to a good mapping website and print out a map of that immediate neighborhood. Then have a "practice run" to each of the clinics so you will know exactly how much time to allow for driving when the need arises. Keep the maps to the vets in the glove compartment of your car.

Common Emergencies and How to Respond

Bleeding Toenail

Whether you've inadvertently clipped a nail too close or your bunny has caught his toenail in something and ripped it from its nail bed, the sight of a foot gushing blood is enough to frighten even the most savvy of pet owners. While this isn't likely to be fatal, it certainly is never good for even a healthy bunny to lose any amount of blood.

Apply styptic powder to a bleeding toenail.

To stop the bleeding, either apply styptic powder or press the nail firmly into a softened bar of soap. Then apply a diluted solution of povidone iodine and try to keep your bunny in as clean an environment as possible. Have your vet do a follow-up check, as a bacterial infection in this area can travel to the bone and cause serious, life-threatening infections. If your bunny is light colored and the blood stains the fur, dabbing it with hydrogen peroxide on a cotton ball or tissue will remove the stain.

When Is It an Emergency?

Sometimes an emergency is obvious, while other times emergency symptoms aren't quite so easy to determine. However, if you see any of the following symptoms, you should call your veterinarian immediately.

- Inability or unwillingness to respond to visual or physical stimulation
- Gasping for air
- Stretching neck and head up (sudden onset pneumonia is not uncommon)
- Seizures/acting drunk/rolling or tumbling
- Severe diarrhea
- Head tilting to side
- Known ingestion of a toxic substance/poisoning
- Elevated or lowered temperature
- Limb dangling
- Unconsciousness
- Obviously broken limb
- Bleeding profusely internally or externally
- Labored breathing
- Lack of coordination
- Abnormal eating or drinking
- Lack of normal urination or defecation for 8-12 hours
- Presence of red blood in normal urine (not to be confused with red urine)
- No weight placed on any limb
- Grinding of teeth
- Sitting in a corner and looking depressed
- Difficulty breathing
- Sound of lungs rattling

Runny Eyes

Runny eyes are not always indicative of a cold. Sometimes it may be nothing more than a foreign object (e.g. dust, dirt, hay, or food crumb) in the eye. You can safely take care of this problem yourself, without a trip to the vet, if you can see the irritant on the surface of the eyeball (or on the outer portion of the lid). Just gently flush the eye with sterile saline and dry the eye area well.

Sometimes the internal duct that runs from the corner of the eye to the nose will become blocked, which will cause a nasal discharge and will necessitate a trip to your vet to be flushed. However, this isn't considered an "emergency" situation, so you can wait until your regular vet is available. If this is a chronic condition, you may have to learn to do the duct flush at home.

Broken Bone

If you think your rabbit has a broken limb and you cannot get him to a clinic immediately, you should do your best to limit your bunny's movement as much as possible. Never attempt to splint or set the bone yourself. Put him in a very small cage or box with food and water very close to him, so he does not have to move to reach it. Either put him in that same cage when you take him to the vet, or wrap him tightly in a towel and hold him against you to limit his movement. Remember that he is in pain, and he may hurt you without meaning to.

A broken bone can heal with good results if it is properly set within a reasonable length of time. If it does not heal properly, amputation may be necessary. Don't be talked into euthanizing your pet because he needs an amputation. Almost every bunny will quickly learn to adapt, and before long he will learn to hop around so efficiently you won't even notice the missing limb.

Severe Ear Problems

Because in some breeds the ears represent a large portion of body area, it is vitally important to keep their ears in good condition. You won't have to wonder if your bunny has an ear problem. He'll tell you with violent headshakes and continuous scratching with his hind foot or pawing with his front paws.

Evacuation Emergencies

Emergencies don't always just concern the rabbit. Sometimes an emergency that will affect your bunny is also going to affect you and your neighborhood as well. Although accidents can happen anywhere (gas line ruptures, propane leaks, toxic spills, etc.) and can cause unexpected evacuations, if you live in an area that is known to be at risk for earthquakes, tornados, hurricanes, forest fires, or other disasters that may require speedy evacuation, you should keep an emergency kit prepared so you can take care of your bunny along with your other family members and possessions.

Micro-chipping and Tatooing for Identification

Most rabbits are tattooed in some manner when they are very young, and most breeders have a code that they use to mark their bunnies so they can be tracked throughout their lives. Make sure your veterinarian has a record of your rabbit's tattoo that can help identify him if he is lost or stolen.

If your pet has not been tattooed, most rabbit breeders have the equipment to do tattoos, and most will be happy to do so for a nominal fee.

If you don't want a tattoo or desire an identification that is more widely recognized, you might want to consider getting your rabbit micro-chipped. As the name implies, a tiny injectable computer chip that carries a unique identification number programmed into it is injected beneath the animal's skin using a regular hypodermic needle that is only slightly larger than one used for normal medication injections. Anesthesia isn't required, and most animals pay no more mind to the needle than they do for normal injections.

There is no scarring, and the chip is completely biocompatible and will not burn or irritate the animal. Once the chip is in place, the animal can be identified for the rest of his life by simply having a special scanner passed over his body that will read the number that will then correlate with owner identification.

You should keep a week's supply of rabbit food in freezer bags in your refrigerator. If you run out of food and have to borrow from the stash, always remember to replace it quickly. Keep a few bottles of fresh water (change the water every month or so) in a large tote bag in the pantry or other easily accessible place. That bag should also include a few of your bunny's favorite treats and a few days' supply of any medication that he takes on a regular basis. If your rabbit isn't tattooed or micro-chipped, you should have that done, and make sure that the vets and shelters in your area have the number on file.

Find an animal-loving neighbor with whom you can plan to work on the "buddy system." In case of emergency, if you aren't home he or she will take care of your animals, and you'll do the same for him or her if the reverse is true.

Your rabbit should be very accustomed to his travel cage, and it should be ready for duty at a moment's notice. If you use the travel cage as a den in his exercise area with the door taken off, the door should be bungeed or strapped to the rear of his cage for easy retrieval in an emergency.

Medication Tip

Although giving a rabbit medication is never easy, some rabbits will more readily take their medicine if their pills are crushed and mixed with a little V8 juice, unsweetened applesauce, or a vegetable baby food.

How to Handle an Emergency Like a Pro

• Stay calm.

• Keep critical information near the phone.

• Know the address and phone number for the vet clinic and your backup vet, as well as the phone numbers for a 24-hour emergency pet hospital, ASPCA Animal Poison Control Center, your pet-sitter, and animal control.

• Educate yourself! Know the signs of a true emergency so you don't "cry wolf" over what might be normal occurrences.

• Be able to discuss your pet's symptoms knowledgeably with the health professional when you call.

Keep a photo of your pet in your wallet, not just for "bragging" but for identification in case you are separated from your pet during a disaster.

Even if you don't plan on traveling in the near future, you should always check out boarding and kennel facilities in your area in case you are evacuated and there is no hotel or human shelter that will allow you to bring an animal with you. Make sure you know where all animal shelters and rescue groups are located in case you are separated from your pet and there's a chance he might have turned up there.

Remember to comfort your animal during any disaster. He will feel your pain and anxiety yet won't be able to be aware of what is really going on. Talk to him, let him know you are there and that he is taken care of.

First-Aid Kit

Any savvy rabbit owner will keep a well-stocked first-aid kit for bunny emergencies. This should include at least most of the following items.

• Large syringe for gently giving liquid medications or for drawing discharge from nose or ears

• Silver nitrate sticks or styptic pencil for stopping bleeding toenails

• Chewable children's aspirins (ask your veterinarian what portion you can give your rabbit for pain)

• Saline solution (or plain contact lens solution)

• Mineral oil or packaged hairball remedy

• Dried lactobacillus acidophilus powder or capsules

• Vegetable baby food, canned pumpkins, or canned vegetable juice

• Hydrogen peroxide (this can remove blood stains from fur)

• Antiseptic soap

• Pedialyte or other electrolyte solution to avoid dehydration

• Cotton swabs

• Adhesive stretch bandage

• Stretch gauze

• Penlight or small flashlight

• Tweezers

• Blunt-end scissors

• Unbreakable thermometer

• Heating pad

• Towels

• Antibiotic ointment for cuts or wounds

• Stethoscope (every rabbit owner should own one)

Rabbit owners should have a well-stocked first-aid kit for emergencies.

Part 3

How To Recognize a Rabbit in Pain

A rabbit that is in pain will usually sit all hunched up, sometimes in a different part of his cage than usual. He will have his eyes half-closed, and they won't appear shiny and alert. The most common cause of pain in the rabbit is a bellyache. Before you call your vet, check your rabbit's litter tray for misshapen droppings, loose stools, or droppings that are strung together with strands of fur. You should also try to remember if your rabbit has been eating and drinking normally up to this point.

Pain Management

Any rabbit that is in pain is a rabbit that needs veterinary attention immediately. Signs of pain in a rabbit include the following.

• Depression

• Excessive salivation

Preparing for Future Emergencies

While your rabbit is happy and healthy is the time to make preparations for the emergency that you can pretty well count on occurring at some time during your rabbit's life.

Make sure you not only have chosen the right vet and a good backup vet, but know both of those vets' schedules! Some vets work only a few days a week or work later on some days. Knowing when they're there can come in handy when you're dealing with an emergency and want to find a veterinarian fast.

Keep the names, addresses, and phone numbers of your vet, your back-up vet, and an emergency clinic beside your telephone. If the vets you chose have offices in areas with which you are unfamiliar, go to a good mapping website and print out a map of that immediate neighborhood. Then have a "practice run" to each of the clinics so you will know exactly how much time to allow for driving when the need arises. Keep the maps to the vets in the glove compartment of your car.

• Frequent grinding of the teeth (Occasional tooth grinding can be normal and in some rabbits is the equivalent of a cat purring. Know your rabbit's usual behaviors.)

• Inability to sleep

• Loss of appetite

• Rapid or labored breathing

• Reluctance to move

• Sitting in a hunched posture all the time (especially if his eyes are half-closed or dull in appearance)

• Unexplained aggression

• Unusual body posture

Remember that rabbits don't like to draw a lot of attention to themselves when they are sick. Your rabbit, in fact, may have been sick for some time before he finally allowed any symptoms to be exhibited. Know your rabbit well so you can recognize the early warning signals of illness, pain, or disease. And don't be afraid to take your rabbit to your vet on a hunch that something might be wrong. It's better to be safe than sorry.

Caring for Older Rabbits

Only a few years ago, most published literature about rabbits stated that rabbits had a life expectancy of only four to five years. This misconception was "proven" by the recorded deaths of pet rabbits; however, these records were based mostly on outdoor rabbits kept primarily for breeding, many of which were neglected throughout their lives. There is no doubt that poor management practices, rich diets, and the lack of spaying/neutering added to the causes for the early deaths of those rabbits.

Today's pet rabbits do not have to meet this fate. With the knowledge we have at the present and the immense amount of education available for pet owners regarding proper health, veterinary

Well-cared-for rabbits can live for as many as 15 years.

A Rabbit's Lifespan

Although older materials about rabbits stated that their life expectancy was only four to five years, there have been documented cases of rabbits living into their teen years. With proper health care, a healthy diet, and exercise, your rabbit can be a part of your family for a very long time.

care, and feeding for house rabbits, you can plan on keeping your beloved pet for as many as 15 years.

Common Problems and Changes in Older Rabbits

You will notice many behavior and health changes in your rabbit as he ages. You will find that rabbits tend to slow down a little after they reach two or three years of age. Most people say that their rabbits become the perfect pet at this age, as they are calmer, more adaptable to different situations, and more loveable as well as loving. Some rabbits need special care as they get older, however, so it's important to watch for many of the changes your rabbit will experience as he ages—some of these changes may signal a problem.

Joint Problems and Arthritis

Unfortunately, after a rabbit reaches the age of six or so, he may slow down considerably due to joint problems or arthritis. Just as older humans notice more aches and pains associated with growing older, the older rabbit will also need to be more careful not to overexercise or overwork himself. It may be necessary to have your veterinarian prescribe pain relievers or other medication. Never medicate your rabbit using human medications, as many can be toxic to rabbits.

You should also let your veterinarian determine where the rabbit's pain is actually coming from, because what appears to be joint pain may actually be masking another treatable health problem. Don't let his joint pain keep him from getting adequate exercise. Keeping your rabbit active will help keep him fit and in good health, and will definitely slow the aging process.

Obesity

Obesity is a major problem for older rabbits and can even prove fatal. Rabbits that are more obese and have more

Keeping your rabbit active will slow the aging process significantly.

"fat wrinkles" are prone to getting fungus and moisture-related skin problems and many heart and kidney illnesses that are commonly linked to being overweight. Rabbits must spend time outside their cage having free run in a large exercise area on a daily basis. A rabbit that is kept confined to a cage, no matter how nice and large it is, will live a shorter (and less happy) life.

It is very important that your rabbit continues a good program of exercise and eat a balanced diet that has been formulated for his needs as he ages. Alfalfa hay is actually very bad for older rabbits. Ask your veterinarian what he or she suggests as an adequate diet for a geriatric bunny.

Dental Problems

Dental problems also seem to plague older rabbits more than young rabbits. Things such as dental spurs on back molars (a problem that vets and owners often overlook) may cause an older rabbit to go off his feed, or it may limit his eating to only softer foods. Make certain that the veterinarian you have chosen is trained to handle serious dental problems in rabbits or can refer you to someone who can. Tooth problems can end up being fatal for the older rabbit if the pain causes him to lose the desire to eat or even live. Rabbits can also starve to death if an owner is not quick to notice the problem. This is why you should be sure to have a veterinarian check your rabbit's teeth on a regular basis.

Overgrowth is also a problem because older rabbits sometimes do not chew as much; therefore, their teeth don't wear down as quickly and efficiently as they did when they were younger. In this case, they will need to be filed or trimmed by your veterinarian. (Never attempt to do this yourself, as it can cause an infection that can be fatal to your rabbit, especially if he is older.)

Have your veterinarian check an older rabbit's teeth often.

Respiratory Problems

Chronic respiratory problems are common in older rabbits, especially rabbits that have a history of respiratory distress signals, including sneezing and nasal discharge. If these problems are not treated aggressively and routinely in the young rabbit, they may lead to lower respiratory infections and the septicemic spread of infection, which can lead to abscesses in other areas of the body.

An abscess is an accumulation of pus that is created by tissue degeneration that forms when infectious agents, such as bacteria, fungus, parasites, or foreign bodies like splinters, lodge in the tissue and cause inflammation. Abscesses can form in any tissue of the body, but seem to be found more often in a rabbit's jaw.

The most common cause of an abscess in a rabbit is usually a bite wound that became infected. Tooth root and tear duct infections also are known to abscess and cause problems that can be easily fatal, because an abscess can rupture internally and cause septicemia before even a savvy rabbit owner realizes there is a potential problem.

Abscesses also seem worse in the geriatric rabbit, especially rabbits that have a history of chronic infections. These abscesses are usually more severe than in younger rabbits and will require surgery instead of just the placement of a drain.

Bladder Infections

Elderly rabbits also will be more prone to bladder infections and stones and may lose the ability to control their bladders. Symptoms of bladder problems include urinating in his bed or other places he would normally try to keep clean, straining unsuccessfully to urinate, or whimpering with pain during urination. By the time a rabbit exhibits pain during urination, it is likely that the bladder stones have become so large that they will not be treatable without surgery.

It is important that you notice the early symptoms of bladder problems before they get to the point that they will be harder to treat. Even bladder stones can be treated without surgery, with the use of fluids and various medications to flush the bladder. Dietary changes may help with incontinence and the avoidance of future bladder stones.

A healthy diet low in calcium helps your rabbit avoid bladder infections.

Many older rabbits die of renal (kidney) failure. Urinary tract infections, kidney and bladder stones, or sludge may make a rabbit more prone to kidney failure. Early treatment and follow-up veterinary treatment is important to keep your rabbit's urinary tract healthy. Feeding a diet that is low in calcium, keeping the litter box clean, and always having lots of fresh, clean water available will go far in avoiding bladder and urinary tract diseases.

Heart Disease

Although heart disease may appear to be sudden in onset in the older rabbit, cardiomyopathy has probably been a pre-existing problem that became visible only when it reached a dangerous point. Acute onset of breathing difficulty may be the only sign of heart disease. A radiograph at that time can show an enlarged heart or fluid in the chest. Symptoms can be treated, but the prognosis at that point is very grave.

Signs of Aging

Old age doesn't have a predetermined moment of onset. Signs of aging may be seen in rabbits as young as four or five years of age in some breeds and not until six or seven in others. The following signs could be indications of old age in your rabbit.

- Decreased activity
- Change in weight (loss or gain)
- Problems with mobility (especially problems with back legs)
- Dental problems
- Urinary tract, bladder stones, or other bladder complaints
- Problems with eyesight and hearing
- Growths on skin or mucous membranes

Obesity is very much a contributing factor of heart problems in the older rabbit, making your rabbit's diet and adequate exercise even more important. You should cut down or even eliminate the pellets in your older rabbit's diet if he is eating the correct amounts of hay and appropriate greens. The House Rabbit Society recommends feeding 1/4 to 1/2 cup of pellets per day per six pounds of body weight, providing the rabbit is getting enough hay and greens for the proper nutritional balance. Just as with humans, obesity is a contributing factor of heart disease. It is even more so in animals. Changing your rabbit's diet simply reduces the risks of obesity that may come with lessened activity as the rabbit gets older. Although you should increase the amount of leafy greens you feed your older rabbit (carrot tops, parsley, cilantro) you should eliminate broccoli, kale, cabbage, or greens that are high in calcium from his diet entirely.

Expanded Veterinary Health Care

Rabbits of all ages should be examined by a veterinarian on a regular basis. By the time they are five years of age or so, however, blood tests and urinalysis should be performed every year for the rest of their lives. If your older rabbit is experiencing decreased mobility,

Part 3

Frequent veterinary checkups are necessary when your rabbit gets older.

pain, or stiffness, X-rays should be taken to check for arthritis or spinal disease that can be treated with medications to make your older rabbit's life better and last longer.

Rabbits start to show old age or geriatric problems after they are about five years or so of age. Therefore, starting a program of extra veterinary care at that time, as well as the special home care mentioned above, can extend the life of your pet and maintain his quality of life amazingly well.

More frequent vet checkups are recommended for senior rabbits, which include a thorough physical exam. Most veterinarians recommend that this should be done every six months. Rabbits can develop illness and disease rapidly–especially the increasingly common cancers, kidney disease, and heart disease–and waiting an entire year between visits could prevent the early detection and treatment, cure, or management of these diseases.

Your vet may also wish to do additional laboratory work such as a blood chemistry profile and/or an X-ray for additional information, particularly if your pet is exhibiting signs of illness. Sedation may be necessary for the X-ray. Make certain that your vet uses isoflurane as the sedative of choice, because it is so much easier on the rabbit's tender system.

After the age of seven, diagnostic testing may have to be done every six months, along with another semiannual exam. These laboratory workups will be invaluable in detecting any disease early and thus facilitating treatment and prolonging your pet's life.

Resources

ORGANIZATIONS

American Rabbit Breeders Association, Inc.
(ARBA)
P.O. Box 426
Bloomington, IL 61702
Phone: (309) 664-7500
Fax: (309) 664-0941
E-mail: ARBAPOST@aol.com
http://www.arba.net/

American Beveren Rabbit Club
Secretary: Pat Vezino
E-mail: rabbits@centurytel.net
http://www.beverens.8m.com/

American Cavy Breeders Association
Secretary: Lenore Gergen
E-mail: McCavy@aol.com
http://www.acbaonline.com

American Checkered Giant Rabbit Club, Inc.
Secretary: Carol Edwards
E-mail: cedwards@harborside.com
http://www.americancheckeredgiantrabbit.com/

American Dutch Rabbit Club
Secretary: Doreen Bengston
E-mail: Dbengt@acegroup.cc AND
Doreen@selco.lib.mn.us
http://www.dutchrabbit.com

American English Spot Rabbit Club
Secretary: Rosalie Berry
E-mail: berrypatch@att.net
http://www.englishspots.8m.com/

American Federation of New Zealand Rabbit Breeders, Inc.
Secretary: Sam Rizzo
E-mail: Srizzo124@aol.com
http://www.geocities.com/newzealandrba/

American Harlequin Rabbit Club

Secretary: Judy Bustle

E-mail: rogrrabbit@webtv.net

http://www.geocities.com/~harlies/index.html

American Himalayan Rabbit Association

Secretary: Errean Kratochvil

E-mail: himi1@yahoo.com

http://ahra.homestead.com/

American Netherland Dwarf Rabbit Club

Secretary: Sue Travis-Shutter

E-mail: Travisdwar@aol.com

http://www.andrc.com/

American Satin Rabbit Breeders Association

Secretary: Clarence Linsey

E-mail: clinsey@mnu.edu

http://www.asrba.com

American Tan Rabbit Specialty Club

Secretary: Virginia Akin

E-mail: tanrbt@aol.com

http://www.atrsc.net/

The British Rabbit Council

Purefoy House, 7 Kirkgate

Newark, Notts, NG24 1AD

UK

Phone: 44 01636-676042

Fax: 44 01636-611683

E-mail: info@thebrc.org

http://www.thebrc.org/

Creme D'Argent Rabbit Federation

Secretary: Travis West

E-mail: cremedargent@hotmail.com

http://www.hometown.aol.com/cdrgentfedration/CDRF.html

Havana Rabbit Breeders Association

Secretary: Julia Rittenour

E-mail: jrpalace@hotmail.com

http://www.havanarba.com/

Holland Lop Rabbit Specialty Club (HLRSC)

Secretary: Pandora Allen

E-mail: ALRSCsec@aol.com

http://www.hlrsc.com/

Hotot Rabbit Breeders International

Secretary: Sheila Spillers

E-mail: hototrbi@yahoo.com

http://www.blancdehotot.com

Lop Rabbit Club of America

Secretary: Jeanne Welch

E-mail: LRCAsecretary@aol.com

http://www.lrca.net

Mini Lop Rabbit Club of America

Secretary: Pennie Grotheer

E-mail: pgrothee@usd250.k12.ks.us

http://www.miniloprabbit.com

National Californian Rabbit Specialty Club

Secretary: Nita Boatman

E-mail: nitabug@colton.com

http://home.who.rr.com/crsc/

**National Federation of Flemish
Giant Rabbit Breeders**

Secretary: Allen Bush

E-mail: secretary@NFFGRB.com

http://www.nffgrb.com/

National Jersey Wooly Rabbit Club

Secretary: Nancy Hinkston

E-mail: yarnitall@sbcglobal.net

http://www.njwrc.bizland.com/

National Lilac Rabbit Club of America

Secretary: Willis Plank

E-mail: prabbits@pathwaynet.com

http://www.geocities.com/nlrca2002/

National Mini Rex Rabbit Club

Secretary: Doug King

E-mail: kingsminirex@msn.com

http://www.nmrrc.com

National Rex Rabbit Club

Secretary: Bill Lorenz

E-mail: REXSECY@aol.com

http://www.national rexrc.com/

National Silver Fox Rabbit Club

Secretary: Judith Oldenburg-Graf

E-mail: silfoxes@iowatelecom.net

http://www.nationalsilverfoxrabbitclub.org/

Palomino Rabbit Co-Breeders Association

Secretary: Deb Morrison

E-mail: MorePals@aol.com

http://www.geocities.com/Petsburgh/Park/4198/

Rhinelander Rabbit Club of America

Secretary: Linda Carter

E-mail: cartersdesert1@juno.com

http://www.angelfire.com/ri2/Rhinelander/

Silver Marten Rabbit Club

Secretary: Leslie Tucker

E-mail: ltucker@silvermarten.com

http://www.silvermarten.com

Internet Resources

Healthypet

(http://www.healthypet.com)

Healthypet.com is part of the American Animal Hospital
Association, an organization of more than 29,000 veterinary care providers committed to providing excellence
in small animal care.

Petfinder

(http://www.petfinder.org)

Petfinder.org provides an extensive database of adoptable animals, shelters, and rescue groups around the country. You can also post classified ads for lost or found pets, pets wanted, and pets needing homes.

Pets 911

(http://www.1888pets911.org)

Pets 911offers a comprehensive database of lost and found pets, adoption information, pet health, and shelter and rescue information. The website also runs a toll-free phone hotline (1-888-PETS-911) that gives pet owners access to important life-saving information.

Rabbit Hopping Organization of America (R.H.O.A.)

(http://www.rhoa.tk/)

This website provides information on how to introduce your rabbit to the sport of hopping. The organization itself is the first of its kind to offer hopping as a sport to all rabbit owners in the United States. Once registered with the R.H.O.A., members will receive a complete set of rules and guidelines pertaining to training and competition.

The Small Animal Pages

(http://www.pet-net.net/small_animals/rabbits.htm)

This website provides rabbit owners with a variety of pet information, chat groups, humor pages, and links to rescue groups and numerous other rabbit-related websites.

VetQuest

(http://www.vin.com/vetquest/index0.html)

VetQuest is an online veterinary search and referral service. You can search its database for over 25,000 veterinary hospitals and clinics all over the world. The service places special emphasis on veterinarians with advanced online access to the latest health care information and highly qualified veterinary specialists and consultants.

Publications

Best Friends Magazine

5001 Angel Canyon Road

Kanab, UT 84741

http://www.bestfriends.com/news/newshome.htm

Friends of Rabbits

Online Newsletter Archive

P.O. Box 1112

Alexandria, VA 22313

E-mail: information@friendsofrabbits.org

http://www.friendsofrabbits.org/newsletters/newsletter.htm

Fur & Feather Magazine

Printing for Pleasure Ltd.

Elder House

Chattisham

Ipswich

SUFFOLK IP8 3QE

E-mail: furandfeather@btinternet.com

http://www.btinternet.com/~furandfeather/

House Rabbit Journal

148 Broadway

Richmond, CA 94804

http://www.psg.lcs.mit.edu/~carl/paige/HRJ-articles.html

Rabbits Only Magazine

P.O. Box 207

Holbrook, NY 11741

E-mail: Danielle@overtureusa.com

http://www.rabbits.com/

The Rabbit Warren Magazine

E81B Daniels Road

Shelton, WA 98584

E-mail: RabbitWarrenMagazine@yahoo.com

http://therabbitwarren.tripod.com/

Veterinary Resources

Academy of Veterinary Homeopathy (AVH)

P.O. Box 9280

Wilmington, DE 19809

http://www.theavh.org

American Academy of Veterinary Acupuncture (AAVA)

66 Morris Avenue, Suite 2A

Springfield, NJ 07081

E-mail: office@aava.org

http://www.aava.org/

American Animal Hospital Association (AAHA)

P.O. Box 150899

Denver, CO 80215-0899

E-mail: info@aahanet.org

http://www.aahanet.org/Index.cfm

American Holistic Veterinary Medical Association (AHVMA)

2218 Old Emmorton Road

Bel Air, MD 21015

E-mail: office@ahvma.org

http://www.ahvma.org/

American Veterinary Medical Association (AVMA)

1931 North Meacham Road-Suite 100

Schaumburg, IL 60173

E-mail: avmainfo@avma.org

http://www.avma.org

International Veterinary Acupuncture Society (IVAS)

P.O. Box 271395

Ft. Collins, CO 80527-1395

E-mail: office@ivas.org

http://www.ivas.org/main.cfm

Animal Welfare Groups and Rescue Organizations

American Humane Association (AHA)

63 Inverness Drive East

Englewood, CO 80112

Phone: (800) 227-4645

http://www.americanhumane.org

American Society for the Prevention of Cruelty to Animals (ASPCA)

424 E. 92nd Street

New York, NY 10128-6804

Phone: (212) 876-7700

http://www.aspca.org

Best Friends Animal Sanctuary

5001 Angel Canyon Road

Kanab, UT 84741-5001

Phone: (435) 644-2001

E-mail: info@bestfriends.org

http://www.bestfriends.com/

Friends of Rabbits

P.O. Box 1112

Alexandria, VA 22313

E-mail: information@friendsofrabbits.org

http://www.friendsofrabbits.org

House Rabbit Society

148 Broadway

Richmond, CA 94804

Phone: (510) 970-7575

E-mail: care@rabbit.org

http://www.rabbit.org/

Rabbit Welfare Association

RWF P.O. Box 603

Horsham, West Sussex RH13 5WL

Phone: 44 08700 465249

http://www.houserabbit.co.uk/

The Blue Cross

Shilton Road

Burford

Oxon OX18 4PF

Phone: 44 01993 825500

E-mail: info@bluecross.org.uk

http://www.bluecross.org.uk/

The Fund for Animals

200 West 57th Street

New York, NY 10019

Phone: (212) 246-2096

E-mail: fundinfo@fund.org

http://www.fund.org

The Humane Society of the United States (HSUS)

2100 L Street, NW

Washington DC 20037

Phone: (202) 452-1100

http://www.hsus.org

Index

Photo Credits